The
afterLoss

For permission requests, write to the publisher, addressed "Attention: Permissions," at Benjamin@Senssoma.com.

Published by Senssoma Publishing

www.theAfterLoss.com

ISBN 978-0-9915397-2-7

Table of Contents

Nothing will ever be the same. Your life has been forever changed.

Grief is uncovering what that change is and where loss is leading you.

Benjamin Allen

Part One: A Personal Pathway through Grief

We have not met by accident. I will hear your journey. We will meet deep within this crossroad of your labyrinth and mine, for it is our common story that I speak, and you have already echoed within me. We will share a brief moment before we venture onto our own individual pathways. We will walk away the better because we have shared this moment. No, we are truly not alone.

Welcome. I have been waiting for you.

Out of the Ashes: Healing in the Afterloss (Introduction)

The experience we will share here in this companion guide is one of great intimacy. Nothing is more tragic than love lost. But love is not lost. Love has changed. Love may have gone missing; life may have gone missing, but love and life are not lost.

This guidebook is a process designed to rediscover what has gone missing and where it can be found. These pages contain touchstones that will guide you into the missing parts of your relationship with yourself, with the ones you will always love, and with the world you live in now.

When people die many believe they go into an Afterlife, life beyond this dimension. I am one of them. I also believe that I was left in the Afterloss, life within this dimension. The world of Before was forever gone, out of reach, just as their Afterlife left me unreachable. I needed a new way of relating to the ones I love that I could no longer physically touch, to the world within me that no longer looked the same, and the world around me in which I no longer fit.

I needed to find the missing parts of me, my relationship with them and the world I live in now. So I began my search in the strange new landscape of my Afterloss.

As I held my eight-and-a-half month-old child, Bryan, his body was going cold. He had taken his last breath just minutes earlier. He was the first of my family to die and my first experience of great loss. It was in those precious moments when he entered the expanse of his Afterlife where I found myself entering the world of my Afterloss.

My wife, Lydia, was to die six years later. We knew she was going to die even when Bryan took his last breath. We also knew she was going to die before Matt, our oldest son, was to die. For years we traveled the depths of our Afterloss together. And when I held her in my arms as her breath was ending and separating from mine, again another love entered her Afterlife, and I was to move deeper into my Afterloss.

Matt was thirteen when he died. For ten years we had known that he, his brother and mother were terminal. For ten years I had wandered the landscape of my Afterloss, loving, living and losing this child, day after day. Every morning I would wake and know that one day he would die. But not today. And we celebrated every day until that day I was left in the darkest parts of my Afterloss. I had lost everything precious to me and once again I went deeper to find what was left of me.

What I found was the expanse of my loss took me deeper into the expanse of my love that had gone missing. The internal terrain of my Afterloss left me in a world of between – between what was and what will be, in a world missing so much of me, so much of us, so much of the world I once knew.

It is a new world in which I dwell, in a world that will never be the world of Before. I will never be the same and I have come to accept that what was will never be again. But in the unfolding of my Afterloss, in the layers and landscapes of this world of between, I have discovered a new way to experience my love for the ones I will always love, a new way of experiencing me and a new way of experiencing the world I live in now. The expanse of their Afterlives continually expands me in the world of my Afterloss. I am perpetually discovering the missing pieces of me that are waiting to be revealed in the shattered sorrow that still takes me deeper and deeper into life, into love and into loss.

In my Afterloss, grief is not linear. The multi-layers of my sorrow take me deeper into places that I never knew existed. My steps go inward, layer after layer, not forward.

Benjamin Allen

What is this guide about?

The very foundation of this guide is this: I believe that with every loss something is taken and something is given. With every death of someone dear to me I find that a part of me goes with them and a part of them stays with me. There will always be a part of me that is missing. Not lost. Missing, and to be found within this new relationship I have with them. And there will always be a part of the ones I love that they left here to be ever unfolding in me.

Let me give you one example of how that part of me lives in the expanse. I have found the epicenter of my compassion lies in this expanse. Where once I felt for someone in their loss I now feel *with* someone as they are living with loss. We touch that common space in an uncommon way. We sit in our own unique Afterloss embracing a common path that stretches across the universe, just as we are.

It was a long time after the last of my family died before I wrote *Out of the Ashes: Healing in the Afterloss*. I didn't want to write it. People would encourage me to share what I had gone through, but I resisted. Finally, there came a point when I could write my experience because I could see that what I was chronicling was *our* experience, our way through loss after loss, life after life, love after love. I wrote from the expanse – the place within me that we all share in the transcendence of loss.

This guide is an exploration into this expansive nature of life, love and loss. Living in loss is a perpetual reintegration process. It is about harmonizing what has gone and what remains into a new relationship with the ones I love and can no longer physically touch, with the world within me and with the world around me. Hopefully, you will find within these pages a pathway to your own reintegration in the Afterloss.

As you venture into your own Afterloss you will be able to see where loss has taken you and what has been taken from you, and what has been left behind for you, what's gone missing and what is there to be found. It is my greatest wish as we meet here, in our own worlds of the Afterloss, that we find the common pathways that unfold into the depths of our healing.

For me, my loss is in perpetual healing.
My love never ends.
My healing never ends.
Loss is a wound that I carry and heal
daily, moment by moment.

Benjamin Allen

TheAfterloss.com

What is true healing?

There was another feature of loss that enclosed me – the fear of moving on. There came a time when what saved me had begun to kill me. I had come to the point where if I didn't move, I would stagnate.

And yet letting go felt like a betrayal. Lydia said, "Don't let him forget me." How could Matt forget his mother? Oddly, when Matt was close to death he asked me, "Do you think you will forget me?" How could I ever forget him?

Out of the Ashes: Healing in the Afterloss (Glass Beach)

Healing is not a lack of pain. Healing is not about 'moving on,' which suggests leaving something or someone behind. Healing is not about returning to a previous way of living, as if loss was something to get over, as if there was something to return to from where loss had left me.

Healing is about being able to still love, not in spite of the losses, but because of the losses, and in the midst of the losses whether there is pain or not.

Healing is about being able to experience all of life and integrate all of me into an expansive new life that has no need to leave anything behind in order to be fully alive today.

Healing is about being able to hold paradox – to hold both loss and love, emptiness and fullness, time and timelessness, in every moment of my life and live a both/and life instead of the fragmented life of either/or.

Grief yearns for healing. And I experience grief and loss as being an ever-unfolding experience of healing. Grief is not something that has a time limit, or for that matter, any limitations at all. In fact, the deeper I go into my Afterloss the more expansive I experience life and love beyond limitations. There are no borders in the Afterloss and there is no limit to how much healing there is to experience.

Everyone grieves differently. Loss has its own rhythm and reason for each one of us. Time is a meaningless construct in the world of the Afterloss and there is nothing linear about loss. A memory can take us to a time long ago, just seconds from reach. No matter how many moments collect into years, any moment can submerge us deeper and closer to the ones we love and we discover another missing part of us that adds to our healing.

This is my experience of healing and what healing means. It is only my experience. You may have a different understanding of what healing means and I want to encourage you to go deeper into what that is for you.

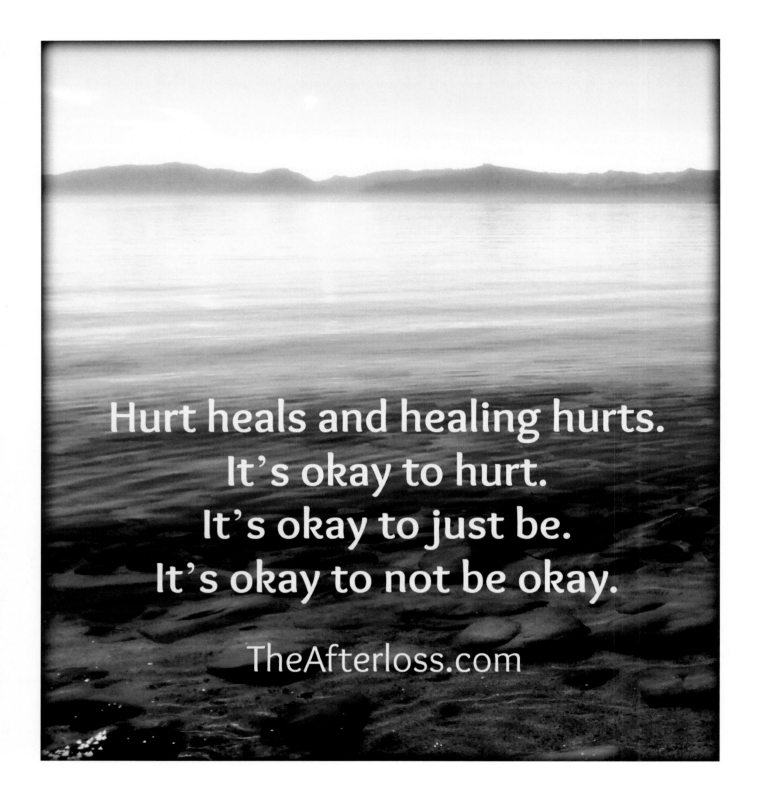

Hurt heals and healing hurts.
It's okay to hurt.
It's okay to just be.
It's okay to not be okay.

TheAfterloss.com

Reflection:

What does healing mean to you? Take a moment to share your thoughts.

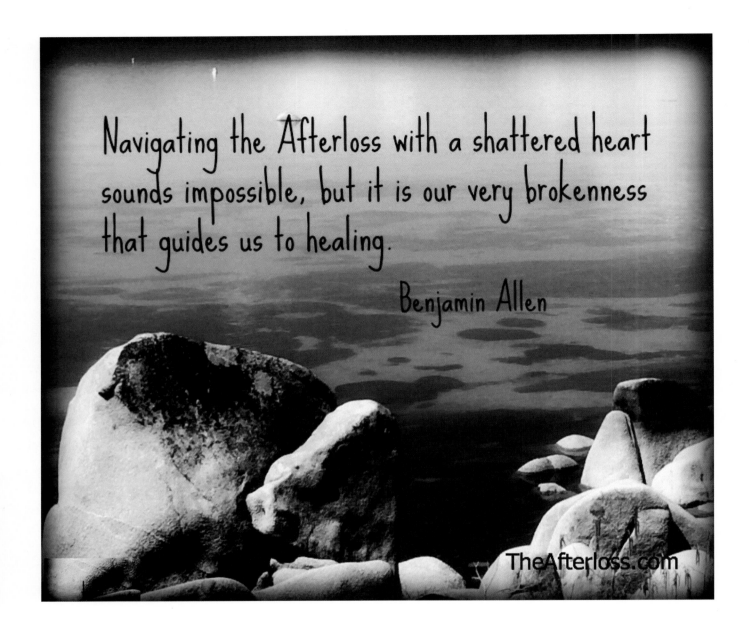

Navigating the Afterloss with a shattered heart sounds impossible, but it is our very brokenness that guides us to healing.

Benjamin Allen

TheAfterloss.com

Give Yourself Permission to be Guided

To get the most out of this process let whatever comes, come. I encourage you to stay out of self-judgment. No question, no feeling, no experience needs to be limited or judged in the scope of your exploration of the deep loss you have experienced and the healing that potentially is on offer. You have been brought here to find a way to live with loss, in spite of loss, because of loss, in the midst of loss.

Much of our pain comes from the resistance to pain. Loss, love and healing can hurt. It is difficult in and of itself to go to those places that are uncomfortable or painful. However, there is no way around the pain. We can only resist it, which creates more pain, or go through the pain to find what awaits us on the other side. I have found that when I go through the emotions I am feeling around loss, they take me to a place of healing. So, I encourage you to lean into whatever comes up and be guided to wherever it takes you.

But if it becomes too difficult, then stop where you are in the emotion and move out of its embrace until you are in a better space to touch those places again. There is no need to force your way through your grief. There is a difference between pushing through the pain and being drawn to a place of healing. Loss is not about creating pain for pain's sake. It is about gently touching those places that have gone missing and finding healing in the midst of the loss.

It is a courageous task to be honest with what you are going through, to lean into every experience loss shapes and to follow loss wherever it leads. I truly believe, that if you do, you will find love waiting where love never left, a beautiful life living here and now that holds then and there in a place of peace, and the underlying love that unfolds and embraces us in every moment and binds us in our common journey – the journey of life, loss and love.

Reflection: What is coming up for you right now?

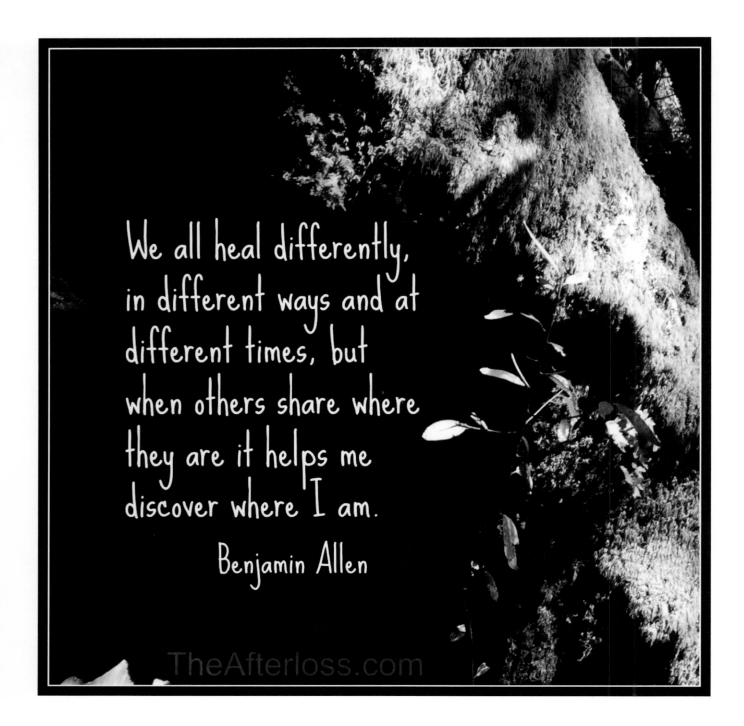

We all heal differently,
in different ways and at
different times, but
when others share where
they are it helps me
discover where I am.

Benjamin Allen

TheAfterloss.com

How to Use This Guide

"Those who have never experienced loss don't know what to say. Those who have, know there is nothing that can be said." ~ Benjamin Allen

This guide is not about giving you answers. It is about giving you an opportunity to find your own answers. Out of your own experiences come the true pathways for you in your Afterloss. I offer you my experiences, but I encourage you to use this guide to go deeper into your own relationship with the one you love, with yourself and with the world you live in now.

I am inviting you on a journey with me. A journey through our shared stories - our stories of loss and our stories of finding the parts of us that have gone missing.

If you've come this far with me, then most likely you've read my book: *Out of the Ashes: Healing in the Afterloss*, but reading *Out of the Ashes* is not a prerequisite for using this companion guide. This is a way to bring more awareness and presence to your own healing.

Here, our stories will intersect. We will meet in this process so we can learn from each other. I'll be sharing some of my own stories, and invite you to bring your own; and together we will weave our experiences into the common landscape of our Afterlosses. There will be questions and exercises within these pages, photographs taken by Rachel Flower and quotes we have used in our Facebook Page, "Grief and Healing in the Afterloss" as well as some quotes from the book to remind you of the stories I shared before. I invite you to capture any insights that come to you as you're reading through this companion guide and then revisit your reflections later if you wish to elaborate on your answers. It will be a kind of real-time conversation between us.

Another way to use this guidebook is to go through it with someone else who has experienced his or her own loss. In this way, you can share your stories and use these exercises to go deeper into yourselves, and with each other.

You might want to get a notebook and pen to carry around with you, so you can jot down thoughts and feelings as they arise. It will help you be more present and engaged with the unfolding of your loss into life.

At other times, when you have an hour or two to spare, you can explore these questions more deeply. Take some time for yourself, and bring yourself to a place where you can be alone and not disturbed, somewhere you feel safe and able to gather your thoughts. It could be a favorite park, your backyard, your bedroom, your deck, or even sitting in your car. Turn off your phone and explore the questions more deeply.

This is a time for you to become aware of the reintegration and renewal process that grief work really is. Take all the time you need.

I used to beat myself up thinking I "should" be able to do more. Gentleness says, "No, this is all I can do and this is all I need to do today."

Benjamin Allen

Be Gentle

Finally, as you venture into this process, please be gentle with yourself. Leaning into loss is not easy.

There are no right or wrong ways to grieve.

We are all doing the best we can. Gentleness comes with an unconditional approach to whatever, and wherever, your loss and life leads you. Be gentle as you touch those places within you that hurt, that heal, that love, no matter if it is in the shape of anger, fear, joy, sorrow, emptiness, fullness…please be gentle.

What we touch touches us and when you touch that part of yourself in this process, touch it with tenderness and love. Whatever you experience is okay. Wherever this process takes you is okay.

You have traveled this far within the massive undertaking of living in loss. And as we meet within these pages know you are not alone. Your footsteps in the Afterloss are uniquely yours, but you will find other footprints along your path. As you gently walk your path, you will find the gentle embrace of others who know the same sorrow, who carry the same pain and who have discovered within it all the same love. You are not alone. We are not alone.

Welcome. Welcome to a place that honors you and knows the courage it will take to go into your experiences of love in search of love's deepest sorrow and greatest joy. It is an honor and a privilege for me to share this time with you and to share our lives together here.

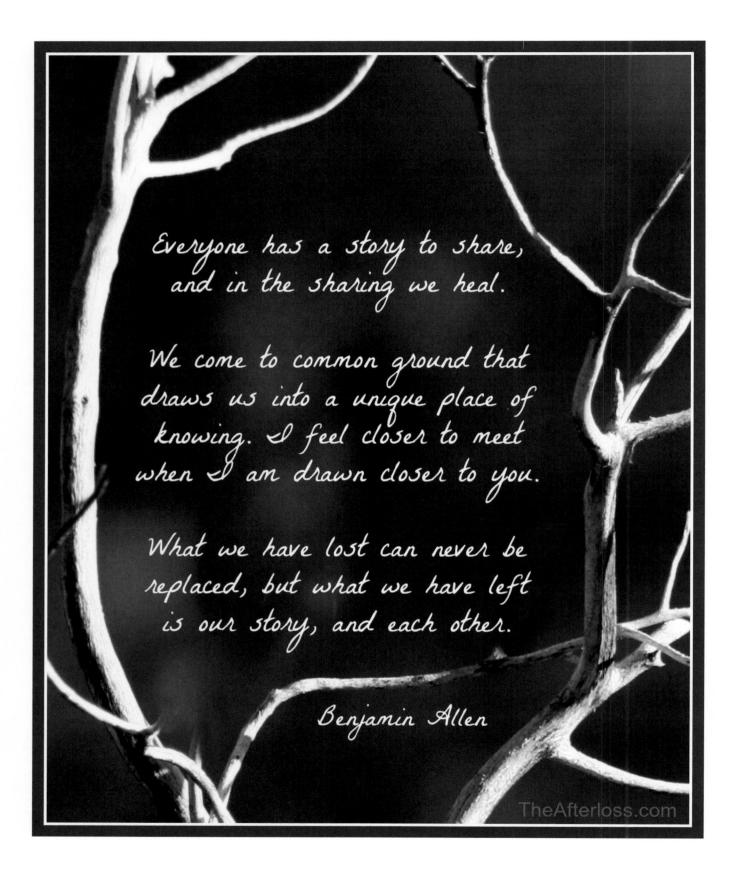

Everyone has a story to share,
and in the sharing we heal.

We come to common ground that
draws us into a unique place of
knowing. I feel closer to meet
when I am drawn closer to you.

What we have lost can never be
replaced, but what we have left
is our story, and each other.

Benjamin Allen

The Stories Behind the Stories We Share

Tell me your story. In the midst of my journey through life and loss, a friend told me a story. It was about a man who had lost his family, his job and his home. The only thing he had left was a rope tied to his neck and he was about to tie the other end to a tree. Another man walked up to him and asked why he was going to end his life. The man said, "I have nothing left." The other man said, "No, that is not true. You have your story."

Out of the Ashes: Healing in the Afterloss (Introduction)

Why do we need to talk about our loved ones with others? Why do we share stories that make us laugh, cry, laugh some more, cry some more? Why is there such a need to have others know the ones we love?

We speak of them because we feel them deep within us. We tell our stories not to keep them alive, but because they are alive. In one way or another, they live within us and we share their lives in story because we still share their lives right now.

Our stories about our loved ones heal us in all realms. We share from the heart to reveal the heart and to renew the heart.

Why does a particular story come to mind when there are so many stories to tell about our loved ones? Think about it. What in a particular story is the story behind the story? We may be telling others about something that happened to or with our loved ones, but there is a reason it is that specific story. There is something of great meaning behind every story we remember, we live and we share.

I believe that embedded in every story told there lies clues to what part of us went with them and what part of them stays with us. We tell stories through the heart and into the heart of this new relationship that is forever unfolding with the ones we will always hold in our hearts.

The following exercises, or reflections, are not about just sharing your stories. Look deeply into the story and see what awaits you there. Feel your story and see where it takes you. Bring the story created in the past into the present and see where it fits in today, guides in today and reveals you in today.

Perhaps this next exercise is the most important exercise in this guidebook. It's importance is two-fold: 1) it is an opportunity to share some of the most meaningful moments you experienced with your loved one, and 2) these stories will guide you into the deeper realms of the Afterloss where you will find more of you, more of them and more of how your world lives in loss and with loss.

We will use these stories as touchstones throughout the guide. Pick three of the most meaningful stories you remember experiencing with your loved one. Often the stories that come to mind are of the most ordinary moments. Sometimes they are big events, but I know for me the most ordinary moments become extraordinary in their remembrance.

Of course, there will be countless "most" meaningful stories to pick from in your lives together. For the sake of this guidebook, choose three so we can go into the various areas and see how these stories unfold you in your relationship with yourself, your loved one and with the world around you. However, feel free to use this process with other stories, other memories made, and yet to be made, with the ones you love and will always love.

Reflection:

Write down three stories that you treasure in your experience with your loved one. It will be helpful if you are able to give each of these stories a title so that it will be easier to refer to each one in subsequent exercises. It might be more helpful to use these same three stories to go deeper as we go, but feel free to change memories and stories if you wish. This is your journey in your Afterloss. Go where it leads you.

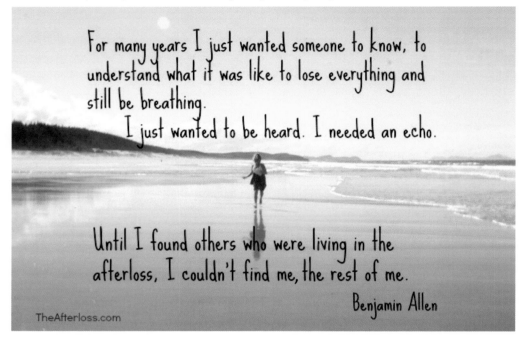

For many years I just wanted someone to know, to understand what it was like to lose everything and still be breathing.
I just wanted to be heard. I needed an echo.

Until I found others who were living in the afterloss, I couldn't find me, the rest of me.

Benjamin Allen

TheAfterloss.com

Story 1 _____

What about this story means the most to you?

What does this reveal about them?

What does this reveal about you?

Story 2 _____

What about this story means the most to you?

What does this reveal about them?

What does this reveal about you?

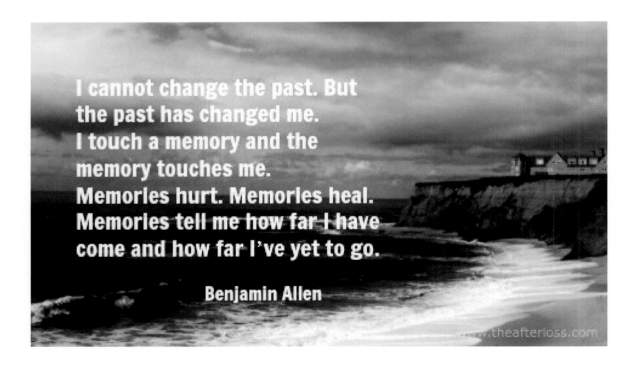

I cannot change the past. But
the past has changed me.
I touch a memory and the
memory touches me.
Memories hurt. Memories heal.
Memories tell me how far I have
come and how far I've yet to go.

Benjamin Allen

www.theafterloss.com

Story 3 _____

What about this story means the most to you?

What does this reveal about them?

What does this reveal about you?

It will take time, but no one
knows how much time.
It will take effort, but no one
knows how much effort.
The only thing we know is grief
will take what it takes.
Benjamin Allen

TheAfterloss.com

Our Four Guides in the Afterloss

It was the promise of continuity I yearned for, some remnant of the covenant between us that might be left behind for me, a timeless token I might hold when I could no longer hold him. All those years I thought if I can just go the distance, there would be something that I would be given to enable me to live when he died. More than anything I wanted to be awake – spiritually, mentally, emotionally and physically awake for the moment Matt woke within the realm, next to Lydia.

Out of the Ashes: Healing in the Afterloss (The Covenant and the Goddess of Wind)

As we enter the experience of traveling through the three major areas of loss focusing on the new relationship with the ones we have lost, ourselves and with the world we live in now, there are four guides that will light the way into a deeper framework and understanding of your own Afterloss. These guides are the physical, emotional, mental and spiritual natures within us that unfold into the way we relate to loss itself. Let's take a brief look at each of them.

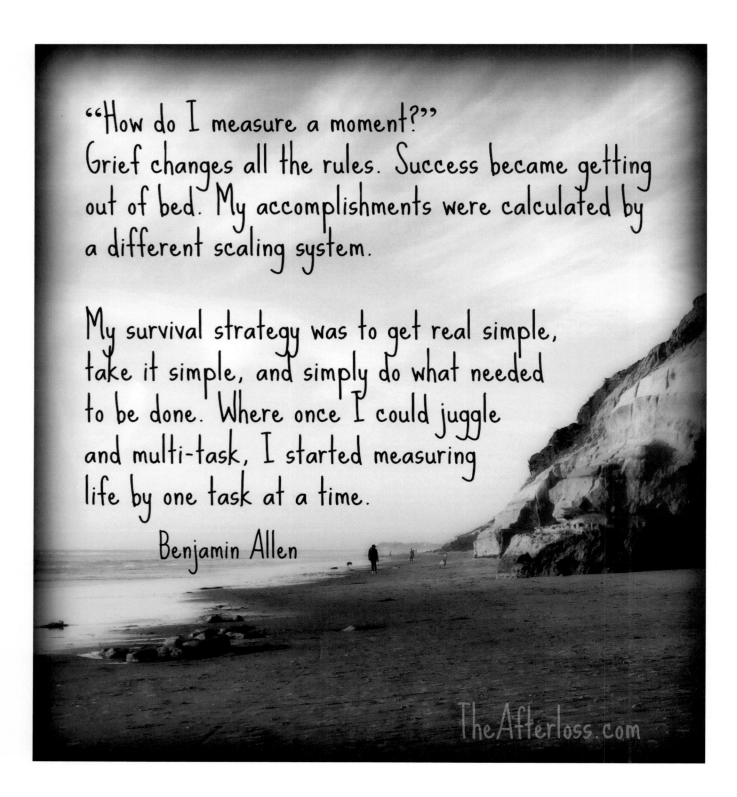

"How do I measure a moment?"
Grief changes all the rules. Success became getting
out of bed. My accomplishments were calculated by
a different scaling system.

My survival strategy was to get real simple,
take it simple, and simply do what needed
to be done. Where once I could juggle
and multi-task, I started measuring
life by one task at a time.

Benjamin Allen

TheAfterloss.com

Physical

There is something unique about our physicality, something precious; perhaps a clue into the wonderment of life that lies within our bodies and this physical manifestation of Spirit. I had been afraid to embrace it because it was a collection of my hurts. To hold what is transitory was to experience the pain of loss. I had looked to transcend the body and its pain and misery, not to hold the body closer in awareness and intentionality.

Out of the Ashes: Healing in the Afterloss (It's Just a Dream)

One of the most pronounced experiences of loss is in the physical realm. The pain of our physical separation of someone we dearly love and can no longer touch is beyond description. From the first day to this day I miss being able to hear their voices, give them a hug, smell the scent of their skin. My oldest child died at the age of 13, but my physical loss entails not just what I lost then, but who he would have been now. I miss not being able to pick up the phone and hear about his life today, in this body, in this moment.

The physical absence of the ones we love and can no longer touch still unfolds in our new relationship with them, with us and with the world in which we live. My relationships with those I have loved in this physical realm, and are now physically unreachable, has not ended upon their deaths. Love does not stop. Life does not stop.

Nevertheless, that physical touch is gone. I will never hold my children or first wife again. This emptiness will be a part of the landscape of my Afterloss for the rest of my physical life. My physical surroundings, within me and around me, have taken on a different shape in the midst of living with loss.

Loss affects us in profound ways physically, and this guidebook is an opportunity to examine how and what we can do to enhance our physical wellbeing in our living with loss.

I have become grateful on those days I simply can't do those surface things. It tells me I'm doing the deeper dance of healing my sorrow.

Benjamin Allen

TheAfterloss.com

What challenges are you facing physically right now?

"There were times when I would go through massive waves of grief... I just had to ride it out. When they subsided it led to an expansion of heart, a deeper way of relating to life and those I love."

Benjamin Allen

www.TheAfterLoss.com

Emotional

I had done a great deal of work on moving through anger, and there was much to move through. Any emotion that solidifies blocks the natural flow of life…

Out of the Ashes: Healing in the Afterloss (What Holds the Body, The Body Holds)

Ultimately, the emotional numbness wears off in the aftershock of loss. Feelings rise, often seemingly without rhyme or reason. But there is rhyme. And there is reason.

Most of us, if not all, feel anger, fear, sadness, depression, guilt, confusion and many other powerful emotions in the overwhelming initial stages of loss. Within the emotional upheaval there are also the possibilities of emotions such as love, peace, gratitude and joy that live in the realm of the Afterloss.

Grief, and our emotions, are not linear. One day could be a day of joy or the fullness of gratitude. The next day could be filled with fear or depression. There is no such thing as "one step forward, two steps back," which many of us have heard said. Grief is "one step deeper, one step to the left or right, and one step deeper still."

Our terminology betrays our belief. How often have you heard or said, "I'm having a bad day?" This reveals our underlying belief that painful emotions are bad. They are not. Pain is part of life and an integral part of loss. Pain is not bad or good. Anger is neither bad nor good. Joy is neither bad nor good. Our emotions are guides to a deeper relationship with life. And I believe underlying all emotions is love. I hurt because I love. I feel because I love. And I heal because I love.

So, this guidebook does not distinguish between good or bad emotions, appropriate or inappropriate emotions, or any other kind of judgment on what someone is going through in the time of great loss. I encourage you not to live in self-judgment for whatever you are feeling as you go through this process, and as you go through life.

The most important element of our emotional state is that we are honest with how we feel, that we are willing to lean into whatever we feel and that we follow our feelings wherever they take us. It is extremely helpful to keep the fluidity of whatever we feel in motion. For I believe every emotion, when embraced in honesty, leaned into and fluidly followed to its end, will end in love.

Therefore, our emotional landscape in the Afterloss can guide us to healing, no matter what the emotion is. And remember, healing is not getting over loss. As stated earlier, healing is about being able to feel all of life and integrate it into an expansive new life that has no need to leave anything behind in order to be fully alive today.

We meet again. And again. And again.
We meet in a song, in an old photograph, a video
that moves over and over, again and again.

I carry more than your picture. I carry your
memory. I carry a moment long ago, just
minutes away in this moment.

Benjamin Allen

Healing in the Afterloss - A Personal Pathway through Grief

What are some of the feelings you experience in an average day?

What are you feeling right now?

Loss is a marathon and
not a sprint.
Many people rise to the
occasion and fall to
pieces in the aftermath.
Loss lasts a lifetime.

The initial shock and
horror that rips a life to
pieces, subsides into the
task of finding what pieces
are left and figuring out
what to do with them.

Benjamin Allen

TheAfterloss.com

Mental

I knew what I didn't believe any longer, but until I let go of it, I would be unable to know what I would come to believe.

Out of the Ashes: Healing in the Afterloss (Empty Words)

When loss shatters us, the mental constructs that we once believed are challenged. Everything is re-examined. The mind attempts to make sense of the senselessness. Questions arise and the search for answers - sometimes to unanswerable questions - begins. How could someone I love so dearly be taken from me? How can life be so cruel? What is left of me now that one of the most important parts of me is missing? The questions of life and loss go on and on, sometimes for a lifetime.

The scope of this guide cannot cover the full range of questions that those of us living in loss live with and seek their answers, but we will touch on some of them. Just as every loss is unique, every journey in loss is unique. Your questions will surface just as your answers will come in the reshaping of your life in the light of your loss. What I hope you experience in this guide is a way to find the questions you need answered and the answers you find that will come uniquely to you within your own relationship with the ones you love and lost, yourself and the world around you.

No question is an exercise in futility, even if there is no answer. All my questions of "Why?" were not in vain. In many cases, I knew there were be no satisfactory answers to some of my questions. Still, I needed to have the freedom to ask anything without reprisal from others or myself.
What I came to see was the questions themselves were an integral part of my healing process. I watched my unrelenting questions become a crucial outlet for my emotional fluidity. My heart would cry out and my mind would search for ways to hold the heart in tenderness as my sorrow lived many a day in its overflow.

Many people live in the protective layers of the mind when their emotions are overwhelming. I experienced this on several occasions and found my wanderings in the Afterloss. The questions, the answers and the unanswerable gave me direction for my emotional upheavals and led me deeper into the interweaving of my emotional, mental and spiritual tapestry.

Please be open to any question that many arise. And I encourage you to be just as open to any answer, including the answer that it is unanswerable.

We all need someone who can find
us when loss leaves us lost.

My search for meaning took me
into some very dark places.

I couldn't find my way out.
Someone had to find their way in.

Benjamin Allen

Reflection:

What questions do you have right now that are in search of answers?

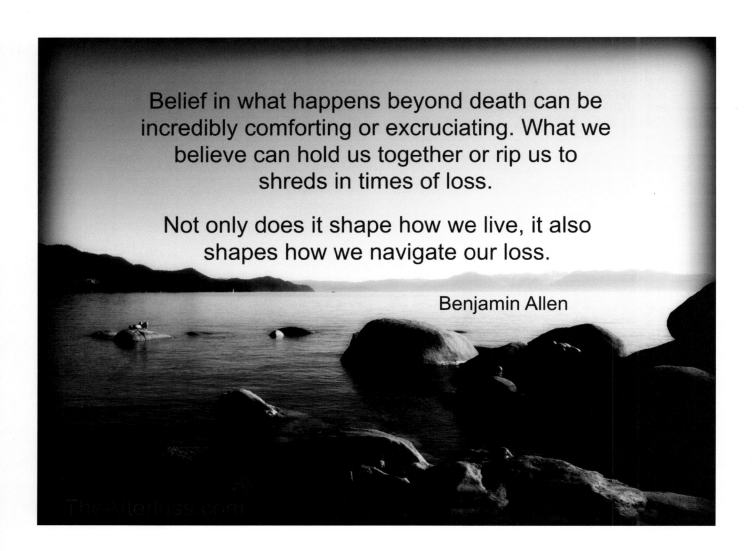

Belief in what happens beyond death can be incredibly comforting or excruciating. What we believe can hold us together or rip us to shreds in times of loss.

Not only does it shape how we live, it also shapes how we navigate our loss.

Benjamin Allen

Spiritual

I watched a tender dance of spirits leaving signatures in invisible ink. Lydia and Matt were more involved in the business of preparing to meet again than saying goodbye. On the surface we prepared a child for the death of his mother. Beneath the surface, mother and child were two spirits preparing for another embrace. A covenant was unfolding.

Out of the Ashes: Healing in the Afterloss (Returning to the Source)

This guide is designed for you to find and/or express the spiritual beliefs that are true to you. The most universal definition of spiritual is "what gives meaning." How you express the meaning within the nature of your being in the midst of loss is crucial regardless of what expression you embrace.

The spiritual aspect of us can be seen as an underlying essence expressed in all of us – physically, emotionally and mentally. It can be experienced as an harmonic essence that keeps us breathing, feeling, thinking and being in this world. Without meaning, without spirit, we die.

This underlying essence can be understood as a transcendent power that clothes life in meaning. Some translate this power into God, Spirit or other names that attempt to describe the indescribable. Others who do not believe in God, Spirit or another name for this power, have their own way of describing the indescribable. But whatever the landscape of your life, and especially in the Afterloss, it is extremely helpful to come to terms with the terms you use and the meaning behind it all.

The most fundamental question of life is death. I have worked professionally with individuals who were close to death and have died. I have sat with families and friends of those who have lost someone dear. I have lived personally in their shoes. And every one of us has this fundamental question – what happens when we die?

I believe all of us live in response to the question of what is beyond death, whether we are a part of a religious tradition, an individual spiritual path or not. I have sat with those who believe nothing is beyond this breath, all the way to those who hold dear a firm belief in a life beyond this life detailed specifically by a religious belief system. I have engaged with those who embrace reincarnation and those that believe there is only one life and it ends in either Heaven or Hell. And I have walked with those from all religious faiths. Each one has articulated to me what they believe happens when we die. And I have observed that each one lives life according to that belief, lives love according to that belief…and lives loss according to that belief.

Spiritual beliefs are most challenged when death takes someone we love, or when we are about to face our own death. What we say we believe is unveiled to reveal what we truly believe in the light of death.

Part of this guide is an exploration of what we truly believe happens when we die. It is about finding meaning in oftentimes the meaninglessness of love that has gone missing. We will explore the shape of spirit in the realms of how we relate now to the ones we have lost, how we relate to ourselves and how we relate to the world around us.

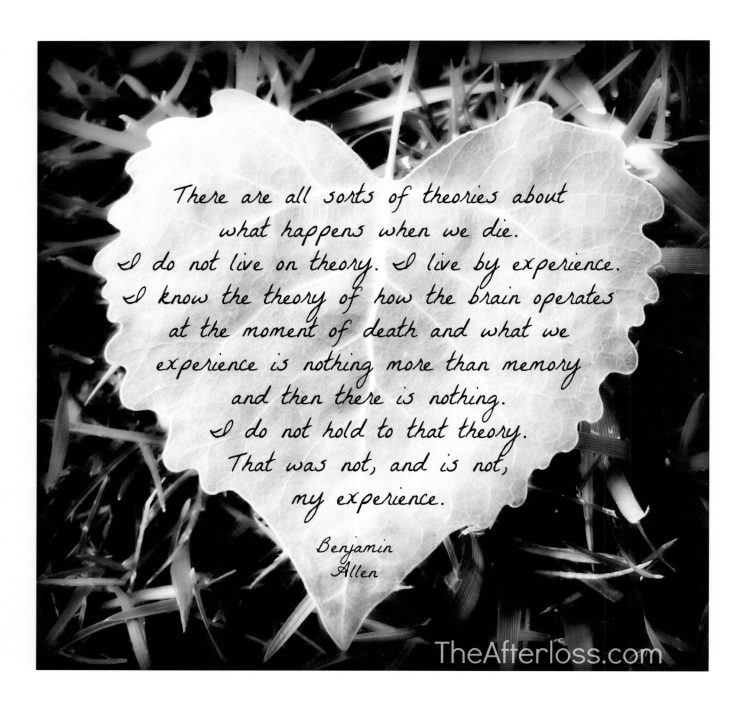

There are all sorts of theories about
what happens when we die.
I do not live on theory. I live by experience.
I know the theory of how the brain operates
at the moment of death and what we
experience is nothing more than memory
and then there is nothing.
I do not hold to that theory.
That was not, and is not,
my experience.

Benjamin
Allen

TheAfterloss.com

Reflection:

What do you believe happens when you die?

There are moments
when I am absolutely
incapacitated. If the
heart did not beat
spontaneously there
would be no beat at all.

In that moment I
measure the distance
by how far am I willing
to go into this pain?

Am I willing to hold the
fullness of love in the
emptiness of my heart?

Benjamin Allen

TheAfterloss.com

Part Two - Our New Relationships In Loss

The second part of this guide consists of three main areas that have been forever changed by loss. They are:

1. A New Relationship with Yourself
2. A New Relationship with the Ones We Will Always Love
3. A New Relationship with the World We Live in Now

Within each of these three areas of loss we will explore four sub-categories. They are:

- ❖ The Physical
- ❖ The Emotional
- ❖ The Mental
- ❖ The Spiritual

Before we go deeper in how we relate now to ourselves, our loss and the world around us, it will be helpful to do a quick snapshot of where you are right now. The following exercise is designed to give you an understanding of what you are going through at this very moment in your physical, emotional, mental and spiritual experience of loss. You may think you know what you are experiencing in these four areas, but when you start writing where you are, it will inevitably take you deeper into where that really is.

Grief isn't linear.
My living in sorrow isn't a progression
of getting better and better.
It's getting deeper and deeper.
The deeper I go the more it looks like on
the surface as doing nothing.
I have become grateful on those days I
simply can't do those surface things.
It tells me I'm doing the deeper dance
of healing the hurt.

TheAfterloss.com

Reflection:

How have your losses affected you physically, emotionally, mentally and spiritually?

Physical Effects

Emotional Effects

Mental Effects

Spiritual Effects

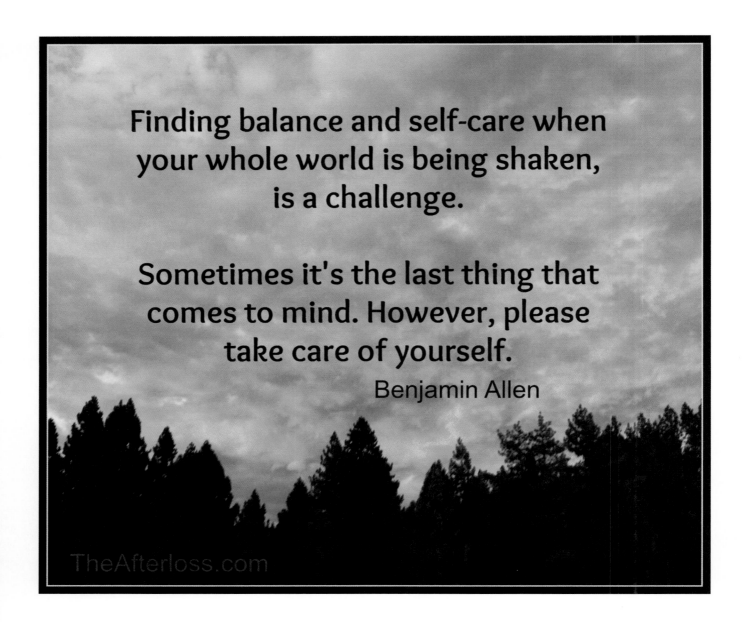

Finding balance and self-care when
your whole world is being shaken,
is a challenge.

Sometimes it's the last thing that
comes to mind. However, please
take care of yourself.

Benjamin Allen

TheAfterloss.com

A New Relationship with Yourself

We each have our own personal labyrinth in the world of the Afterloss, filled with highs and lows, meaning and meaninglessness, life and death, dishes in the sink and unmade beds.... We have within each of us the dark places and the yearning for light. It is part of the human condition to yearn for love, to dream, to live in spite of broken dreams, to manage within the slipping of time and the confinement of space. We hope. We laugh. We cope. We cry. Who am I? Why am I here? Why is this happening? What is my purpose?

Out of the Ashes: Healing in the Afterloss (Introduction)

Loss changes everything. Who we were is no longer who we are. So who are we? What have we become? More importantly, what are we becoming?

As mentioned earlier, I believe that when someone I love dies, a part of me goes with them into the expanse as if I am stretched across the universe in a dimensional time warp. Unraveling what it means to be unraveled is part of that integration process.

We become different people. At some points I needed to contract, to push the world away. The empty space within me was so vast I could hold nothing but the emptiness itself. I gave myself permission to feel and experience what was taken from me, and in the process of being honest with my pain, leaning into my pain and letting my pain take me wherever it led, it led me to that part of me that lives in the expanse.

And the only way I know to get here is to go through there. No matter how much it hurt I held onto the belief that if I just followed the hurt wherever it took me, it would take me to healing. It would take me to that place in the expanse where I could live with the pain in the midst of peace, in the midst of loss, in the midst of love.

I encourage you to be where you are, wherever that is, without judgment. Whatever you find, lean into it, follow it, see where it takes you. What you are following is your pathway through your Afterloss. What you are looking for is that part of you that has gone with them. What you will find is that part of you that resides beyond loss and within love. No matter how much it hurts, lean into those empty places within yourself to find the fullness there.

The following exercises are designed to help you understand how this new relationship with yourself is there to help you in your unfolding. In my experience, this unfolding is a fluid lifetime process. As long as I live I will live with loss, and I will live in love. The expansion of me that has occurred because they were in my life one way and now are in my life another way continues to grow.

Nevertheless, I miss them. I miss what used to be me. I still miss what is gone. Nevertheless, love forever calls me and I will forever follow her echo in the missing parts of me.

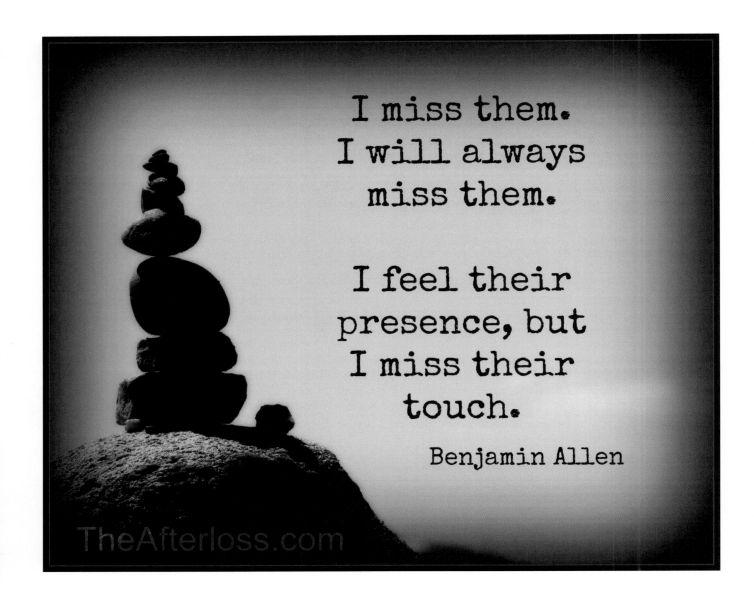

I miss them.
I will always
miss them.

I feel their
presence, but
I miss their
touch.

Benjamin Allen

TheAfterloss.com

Reflection:

What do you miss most?

What seems to have gone missing in you?

What is new or different about you?

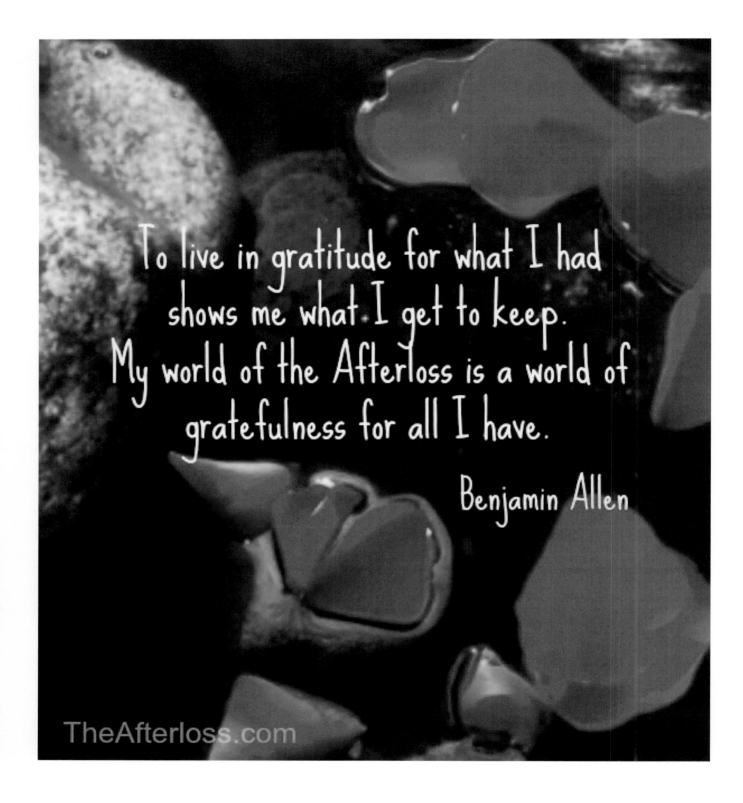

To live in gratitude for what I had shows me what I get to keep. My world of the Afterloss is a world of gratefulness for all I have.

Benjamin Allen

TheAfterloss.com

What Did They Leave You?

I thought it was the big stuff that makes "the" memory, but the pictures pasted in my collage are of the ordinary moments: waking next to her, laughing, driving down a highway, taking Matt to the park. The "un-special" became extraordinarily special. In the last three months of Lydia's life we built a collage of moments that had settled into peace. Memory smoothed the rough edges and we sat in an extraordinary ordinariness.

Out of the Ashes: Healing in the Afterloss (Final Wishes)

Another dynamic of the reintegration is coming to terms with what the ones who have entered this Afterlife have left me in my Afterloss. I will always carry a part of them in me, but where in me and how in me?

The word legacy is often used when referring to what someone has left this world. One definition of legacy is "something from the past that is handed down." In our shattered loss, some of the pieces we pick up and put back together are more than just ourselves. In many ways we a part of their legacy.

We carry within us our loved ones, and how we carry them shapes us and becomes a part of us. There are qualities and characteristics that are incorporated into who we are and how we relate to life that directly come from our loved ones. This can occur consciously or unconsciously.

Reflection:

What did your loved one leave behind? It could be positive or negative, or both.

Do you notice acting or thinking in ways that your loved one once did? If so, what are some examples?

The only way for me to get to my healing was to go through my pain.

I unclenched my life, and as I opened to whatever came, in came the gentleness of grief.

What I thought was going to kill me as actually what was going to heal me.

Benjamin Allen

Who Are We Now?

Can life simply be about shared story? Does the story even matter or is it the collective meaning that binds us? Is our first breath a question mark? And if we choose to live life to the fullest, can our last breath be an exclamation point?

Out of the Ashes: Healing in the Afterloss (Introduction)

Many times people unconsciously take on some characteristics or beliefs of their loved one. I remember standing on the cliffs in Northern California next to the ocean. Lydia died three years earlier. I was alone, emptying what was left of me into the moments that emptied me.

As I stood next to the ocean, a cool wind came to land from the summer sea and brushed against my body. My instinctual reaction was to slightly clinch in the coolness. A thought of discomfort crossed my mind. Then I realized that it was Lydia that didn't like the cool wind. I rather enjoy the ocean breeze. I started to chuckle to myself. In a small way, I was taking on Lydia's persona. That part of her had become in some ways part of me.

This is just a minor example of what goes on beneath the surface in the subterranean world of the Afterloss. Major shifts are happen all the time in a world that is working through the major upheaval of what has gone missing and what is left to reassemble.

Life, loss and love are in flux. We do not lose who we are, but we have an opportunity to expand who we are with the unfolding of our grief and the ever-unfolding of our love for those we can no longer physically touch.

Reflection: The following exercises will help you reclaim who you are now. Even though we are going to explore that part of you that they have touched, that is not entirely who you are as a person. Loss itself touches our core, but these exercises are about finding what is core to you and the very core of you. This entails all of you, which is more than just the relationship with the one you love.

Story 1 _____

What were the qualities you see in that story that expresses the one you loved?

What were the qualities in you that surfaced in the story?

From this specific story, what part of them has become a deeper part of you?

What part of you feels it has become a deeper part of them?

Story 2 _____

What were the qualities you see in that story that expresses the one you loved?

What were the qualities in you that surfaced in the story?

From this specific story, what part of them has become a deeper part of you?

What part of you feels it has become a deeper part of them?

Story 3 _____

What were the qualities you see in that story that expresses the one you loved?

What were the qualities in you that surfaced in the story?

From this specific story, what part of them has become a deeper part of you?

What part of you feels it has become a deeper part of them?

Healing
sometimes hurts.
When I lean into
the hurt I find
my healing.

Benjamin Allen

TheAfterloss.com

Our hearts were insperarable.
Our love still is.

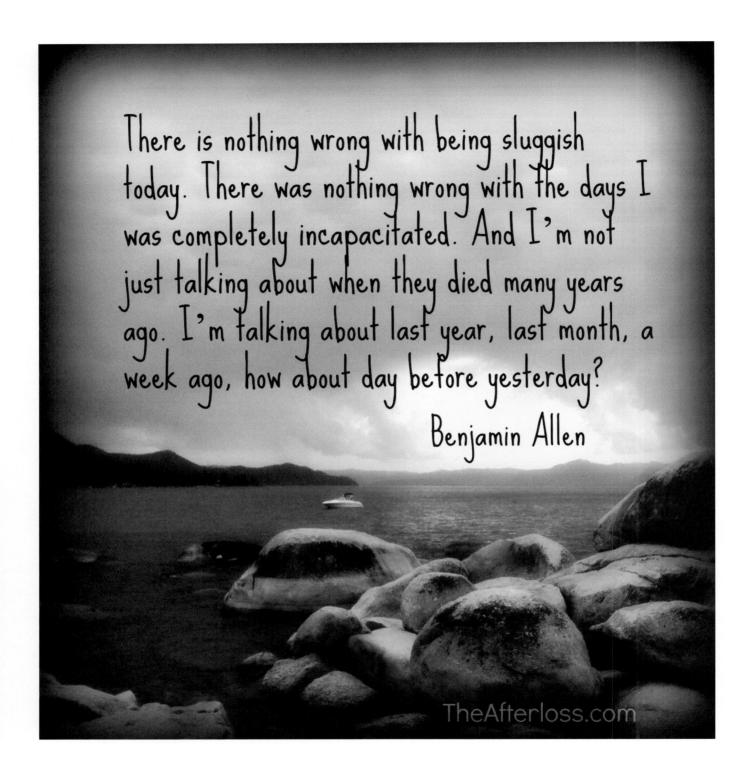

There is nothing wrong with being sluggish today. There was nothing wrong with the days I was completely incapacitated. And I'm not just talking about when they died many years ago. I'm talking about last year, last month, a week ago, how about day before yesterday?

Benjamin Allen

TheAfterloss.com

The New Relationship with Yourself - The Physical

At times, without warning, loss would overwhelm me. I would find myself utterly immobilized or only able to do the simplest of tasks. It could strike anywhere and at any time. A song on the radio would trigger my unfolding. A candle flame could send me back to the candlelit nights by Matt's bed. A box of cereal at the store could drop me into another layer. Loss brought everything into question. What once made sense no longer did.

I was no longer the me I was. I felt like a skinless spirit looking for something to hold me together. One friend came to my house after I'd been in Mendocino for several months. He said, "Some of us are really worried about you. You need to get back into life. What do you do all day?"

I said, "I don't know, but it takes me all day to do it."

Out of the Ashes: Healing in the Afterloss (The Unfolding of Me)

Our physical bodies absorb everything we encounter. What we touch touches us and settles in all of us, including our bodies. How we hold what we feel, believe and experiences can give us clues to how well we are dealing with loss. The following exercises will give you some insights into what you are physically going through and how it is affecting you.

Grief can be extremely exhausting physically. Be aware that the physical depletion of loss is very common. Many of us try to compare what we could do to what we are able to do now and think something is wrong, but nothing is wrong. I look at times when I am not able to do more physically as an indication that there are other areas of my unfolding of loss that require that energy either emotionally, mentally or spiritually. And I have learned that I do what I can…and that is enough.

However, it is absolutely essential to take care of your body. Our emotions, mind and spirit cannot land if there is no place to land and if your body is not available then how can any part of you find healing? It is often extremely difficult to take care of your physical state when the separation, hurt and devastation are so overwhelming. Sleep is hard to come by. Food intake is so difficult to gage. Exercise can become a foreign concept. Nurturing activities for yourself can be neglected with the utter depletion and exhaustion of sorrow.

In the initial stages of loss, life is lived in centimeters and seconds. Then, it transposes into inches and moments, ultimately transcending into larger measurements of time and space. Nervertheless, the weight of a memory or moment could unexpectedly give way to centimeters and seconds again in a flash. This is why monitoring and maintaining a structured plan for eating, exercise, nurturing activities and other aspects of our physical well-being is so important.

For instance, my exercise is something that I do on a regular basis. Not only does it help give me energy and physically feel better, but it enhances my emotional, mental and spiritual states as well.

After Bryan died, I started going to the gym. We only had three months with him after we got the word that he, his older brother and his mother were terminal. I had so many emotions flying around, one of the main ones being anger. I needed a way to constructively release my anger and so I went to the gym every day and channeled it there.

After Matt died, I was alone in the depths of the deepest grief imaginable. Bryan had died. Lydia had died. And now Matt. I could barely get out of bed. I needed to find a way to make it through a day because I felt there was nothing left of me.

I had to inch my way through a day. Getting out of bed was a major victory. Taking a shower, eating, all the normal things under normal circumstances became a challenge. I needed a daily structured plan that guided me from one moment to the next.

Walks by the ocean, compelling myself to meet with friends even though I wanted to be alone, eating even when I didn't want to, and exercising daily no matter how depleted I felt were part of my daily routine. Centimeter by centimeter, inch by inch, moment by moment, the day became days. I needed to be gentle and simple in those centimeters and inches, but I need a structured plan to get me from one moment to the next.

Lydia once said, "I feel like I am walking in a blizzard and if I stop I will die." After they all died I was in my own blizzard. One simple step led to the next simple step. It was all I could do, but it was enough for that moment, that day.

I no longer knew who I was.
I just didn't know who I had become.

I knew what used to be normal. I just
didn't know what the new normal was.
All I knew was I didn't know any more.

Benjamin Allen

TheAfterloss.com

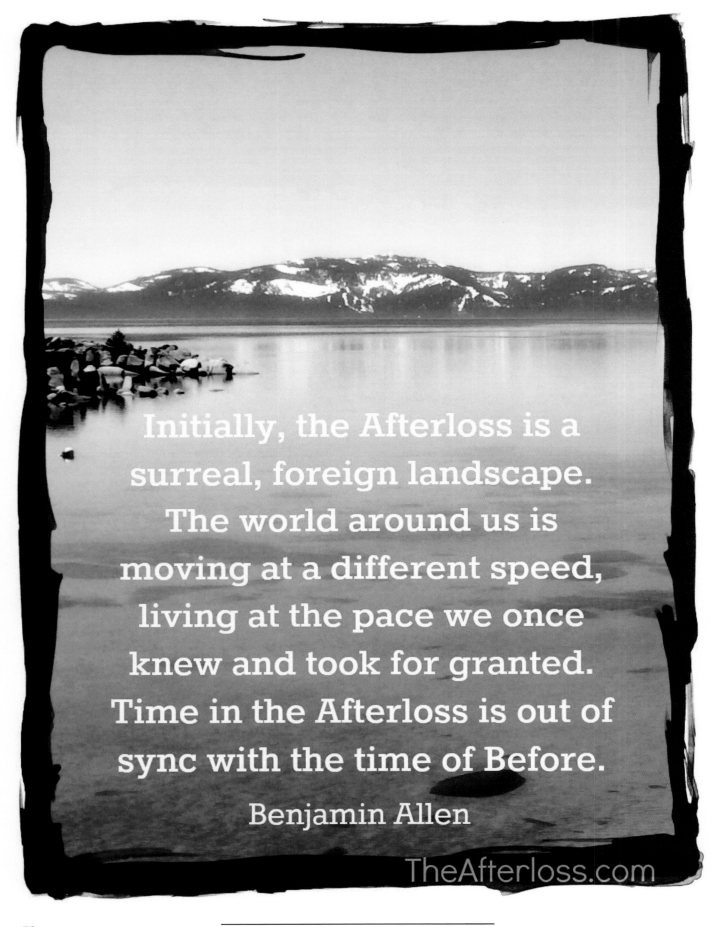

Initially, the Afterloss is a surreal, foreign landscape. The world around us is moving at a different speed, living at the pace we once knew and took for granted. Time in the Afterloss is out of sync with the time of Before.

Benjamin Allen

TheAfterloss.com

Some ideas for taking care of yourself.

- *Daily exercise*
- *Bring yourself to a favorite place*
- *Take a stroll in nature*
- *Shower or bathe with fragrant oils or scented soap*
- *Indulge in a favorite hobby*
- *Listen to soothing or uplifting music*
- *Wear something you love*
- *Enjoy a favorite meal or beverage*
- *Get a massage*
- *Talk with a good friend. Ask for their support in helping you keep a routine for yourself.*
- *Read something upliftiny*
- *Indulge in a favorite hobby*
- *Take a stroll in nature*
- *Watch the sunset*

Write down some of your own ideas whether you are doing them now or not...

What are the ways you feel you are taking care of yourself physically?

What are some areas you feel you would like to improve your physical self-care? How?

Make a plan that includes all of the ways you want to provide physical self-nurture and self-care each day.

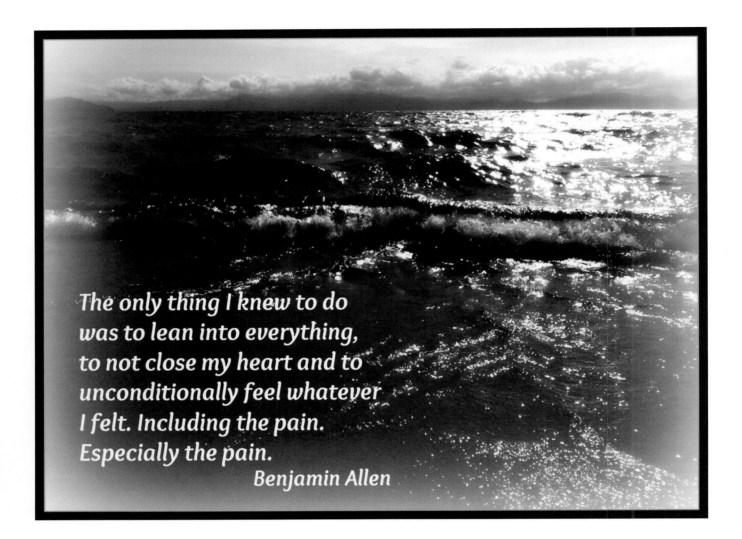

The only thing I knew to do
was to lean into everything,
to not close my heart and to
unconditionally feel whatever
I felt. Including the pain.
Especially the pain.
                    Benjamin Allen

The New Relationship with Yourself – The Emotional

There were times in Mendocino when I would curl tightly into a fetal position, grip my chest and be completely unable to breathe. The impulse would come out of nowhere, but it usually occurred at home. A massive wave of sorrow would engulf me and I just had to ride it out. It would last for about three or four minutes, but it felt like an eternity of hell. I would remember Sandy's words, "Hold your finger in the middle of your heart and never let it close." I would try to do both and breathe at the same time. The moment would subside. My red face began to pale. My body relaxed and I would wipe the tears away. Every time I went through this involuntary convulsion of loss, every time I kept my heart from closing, I always, always walked away with an expanded heart. I opened just a little more and consequently I experienced the world more lovingly. Every contraction offered me an expansion.

Out of the Ashes: Healing in the Afterloss (An Innocent Heart)

No one who has experienced deep loss needs to be told about the emotional devastation. Like waves crashing against the ocean cliffs, every emotion pounds us when loss first happens. Anger, guilt, fear, and numbness are often the first waves that slam against our shattered hearts. Loss brings all that is into the forefront of our emotional state. There is nowhere we can hide from our emotional upheaval.

Loss hurts. Love hurts. Everything hurts when loss takes everything dear to us. We hold on to what was because we feel so much of what we have now is gone. But not all is gone.

The entire spectrum of emotions and their intensity rise and fall and rise again and again. Emotions don't just come and go. If only it were that easy, that simple, that clean. But it is not.

Feelings can rise out of nowhere like a spontaneous combustion. Other feelings are like a perpetual humming background noise that lies just beneath the surface of the day.

All of our feelings, be they anger, guilt, sadness, love, peace, gratitude or any other feeling along the kaleidoscope of emotions, shape who we are and how we relate to life. The numbness of not knowing how to feel because it is so overwhelming, eventually gives way to wave after-wave of emotions.

No emotional state is wrong or damaging in and of itself. What has the capacity to damage us is how we channel (or not channel) our emotions. Every body of water needs both an inlet and an outlet to be healthy. We, too, need to find healthy ways to let our emotions in and let them out. The first part of this exercise deals with where you are right now. The second part will cover what ways you can find to let your emotions stay fluid and find their way to a place of healing. These exercises will help name those feelings and see how you use those feeling in the shaping of your new relationship with you.

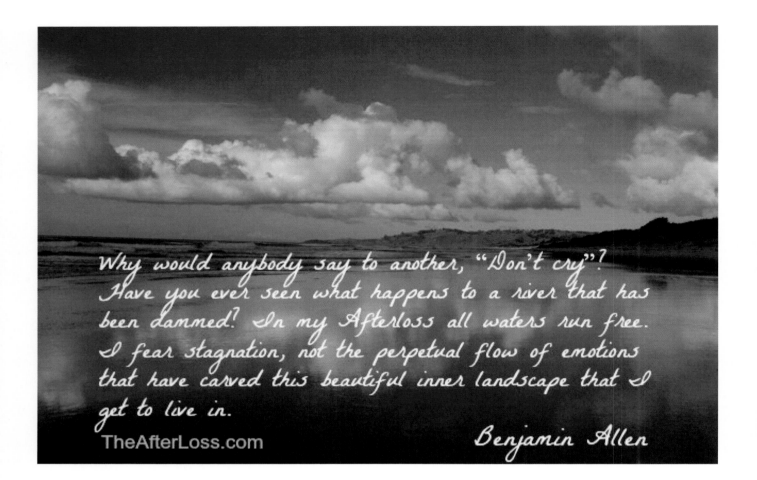

Why would anybody say to another, "Don't cry"? Have you ever seen what happens to a river that has been dammed? In my Afterloss all waters run free. I fear stagnation, not the perpetual flow of emotions that have carved this beautiful inner landscape that I get to live in.

Benjamin Allen

TheAfterLoss.com

Reflection:

1. *What are you feeling right now?*

2. *What emotions rise when you think about the one you love and will always love?*

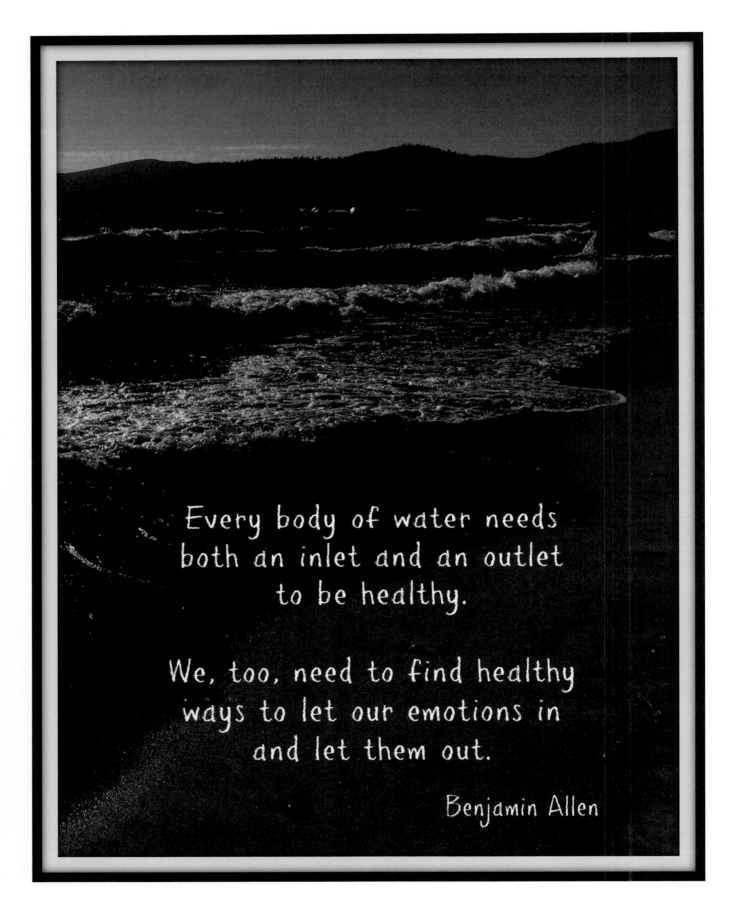

Every body of water needs
both an inlet and an outlet
to be healthy.

We, too, need to find healthy
ways to let our emotions in
and let them out.

Benjamin Allen

3. *What challenges are you experiencing with your emotions?*

4. *With the emotions you identified earlier, what are the healthiest ways you can express them?*

5. *What are some of the ways you can feel your relationship with your loved one today?*

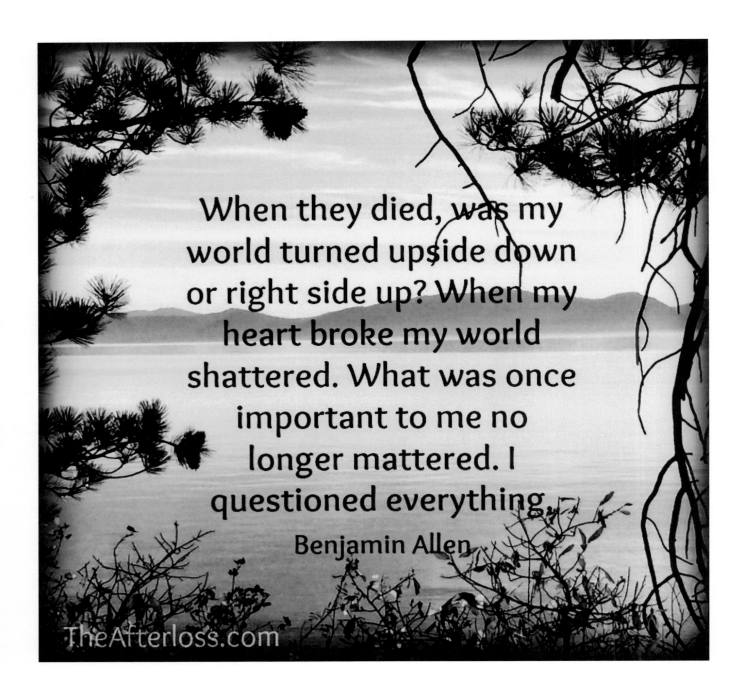

When they died, was my world turned upside down or right side up? When my heart broke my world shattered. What was once important to me no longer mattered. I questioned everything.

Benjamin Allen

TheAfterloss.com

The New Relationship with Yourself - The Mental

What we believe about ourselves and what we believe about life is challenged in loss. Some beliefs are reinforced. Other beliefs can crumble. But all beliefs are re-examined in the light of loss's darkness and light.

The following exercises are an opportunity to touch those beliefs in a different way. Looking into the landscape of your Afterloss, beliefs are seen in a unique light uniquely yours.

The mind seeks understanding. The question "why?" is one of the passageways in the Afterloss that most, if not all, travel. Everyone comes to their own conclusions and touches their own individual landscapes in the Afterloss. The journey through "why?" to its destination is just as unique.

Why didn't they detect the toxemia during Lydia's pregnancy and instead of sending us home kept her in the hospital? Why did Lydia have to have the precautionary transfusion that carried the HIV when she didn't need it? Why did Matt have to get infected with a transfusion just 10 hours before his birth? Why did the blood bank not find us before Bryan was born and he had to endure 8 months of anguish and pain?

The question "why?" is more than some futile outpost in a wasteland of no answer. Why would such love be severed when love is the greatest yearning a human possesses? Why did…? Why would…? Why is…?

Underlying every question of "why" is a plethora of other questions laced with pain. The mind can either heal or hurt us; or the mind can get into a torrent spin cycle that never finds healing. Like the children's game of asking why to every answer until we end up saying "Because!"

But the mind can also be a conduit for healing. The healing nature of the mind, the questioning, the mental unpacking of our attempts to construct some sense out of such devastating loss, occurs when the question includes the heart.

All of us hurt; and it takes all of us to heal. Behind every question is the beat of a broken heart. The mind beats, too. And the pulse of our search for sense in the senselessness, when combined with the beat of the heart, guides us deeper and deeper into the reflective oases of our Afterloss that reflect us. When the mind finds harmony with the heart, we can travel into any question and find the resonance of spirit (i.e. meaning).

So, in many cases, it is not the answers to our question that will create solace in the sorrow. Often, the question is the answer and our solace. And it is the question itself that leads us to healing when it is combined with the heart and rests in spirit.

As stated earlier, please give yourself permission to ask anything and not judge what questions and/or answer arise. Be courageously gentle with yourself as you explore who you are now in your Afterloss through the following exercises.

Reflection:

What unanswered questions do you have in the midst of your loss?

What do you believe, feel or think now?

Are there beliefs you once had that have changed or in the process of changing? What are they?

How can you express the beliefs you hold now in you life?

Just as blood rushes to the heart when physical trauma occurs, spirit collects in the same way during grief. Non-essentials melt away.

Benjamin Allen

TheAfterloss.com

The New Relationship with Yourself - The Spiritual

A brown fallen leaf lay inches from my boot. The extent of its life and the age of its death were unknown to me… I placed the leaf in the forming pool, close to the outlet that trickled down a newly shaped stream…I watched without interference as she rounded the makeshift corner and entered the creek that became a river. She sped down the river's flow to a sea miles away. And just like Matt, a brown leaf left me with only memory; the moment was gone, just the echo remained….

A brown lifeless leaf caught in a torrential downpour in the middle of a forest of rain was my lens of Spirit. Its travels taught me the sacred simplicity of grief's gift.

My soul turned in the direction of the Mysterious Pass and on a journey. There was nothing that could not teach me. I had lost my greatest teacher – my son Matt, but another teaching had commenced.

Out of the Ashes: Healing in the Afterloss (Sound is But an Echo)

What gives meaning? Where do you find meaning in the seeming meaningless of loss?

Using the definition of spiritual we used early as "to what gives meaning," here is a time to address who you are in the context of what is meaningful for you. You may have a particular religious belief where your meaning is expressed. There may be a spiritual path that you hold that isn't tied to any particular religion. You may believe there is nothing of a transcendental nature that works for you. No matter the belief, whether it is a belief in God, in an undefined source or in some other construct, all of us are in search of meaning and in a meaningful search for how loss has shaped us.

More than needing to know "Why?" I needed to know "What now, in the light of who am I now?" After Matt died, the last of the three, I moved to the coast of California. I was no longer a father, a husband, an employee…. I was no longer all those things I had identified myself as, and I was left with the question of "Who am I now?" What I found was within the labyrinth of who I was no longer, who I was, and who I was becoming was the underlying question of "What now is my meaning. What gives meaning? Why am I still alive?"

I literally had nothing left to hold on to and I would walk the forests of my Afterloss looking for what was holding on to me.

All I had left was my loss. It was in this dark forest I decided I would follow loss wherever it led – physically, emotionally, mentally and spiritually. I would lean into every experience without resistance. No matter how much it hurt I would follow loss into its deepest caverns and its highest vistas of my Afterloss.

Leaning into loss unconditionally became my meaning. And it unveiled the kaleidoscopic lens of spirit that crystalized Spirit itself. I began to see everything through this lens. And as I followed every tributary of loss I found myself going deeper into layer after layer of loss, of love, of life and of healing.

The following are exercises designed to help you flesh out what is meaningful for you. What pulls you out of bed and propels you into another day. And, if it fits your belief system, what gives meaning to your moments and helps you in the midst of your loss.

The best way to prepare for the next moment is to live fully in this one.

Benjamin Allen

Reflection:

What gives you meaning?

What spiritual beliefs comfort you?

Are there any spiritual beliefs you feel are harming you?

What are they?

What are ways you can heal within your spirit/meaning?

Conclusion

This new relationship with yourself after loss is a challenge. We will never be the same. We lose so much of us and gain so much of our loved ones. This reintegration process happens on all levels and in every aspect of us, especially the physical, emotional, mental and spiritual parts of us.

We can no longer hold on to what was and what we were. This is just the beginning of discovering what is and what we have become…and are becoming.

Reflection:

What do each of these stories represent in possible changes you are experiencing in your physical, emotional, mental and/or spiritual relationship with who you are today?

Looking back at the three stories, what is the meaning for you that speaks to you from each story?

Story 1 _____

Story 2 _____

Story 3 _____

I feel their presence around me often, but I feel their presence within me always.

Benjamin Allen

A New Relationship with the Ones We Will Always Love

The Rose Ceremony

Red. The color of the heart. I brushed my finger along the thorns of Matt's rose....

I was careful to tear the first red petal at the bottom to ensure the whole petal would release into my fingers. The soft thickness and rich hue of red did not go unnoticed. I encircled her with my fingers and held her at eye level. The wind stole her fragrance, but left a memory. My lips lingered against her softness. I thanked Matt for being my teacher, for widening me by becoming flesh. I kissed the rose petal again and let her go.

The sea engulfed her too quickly. Red disappeared, joining lavender and yellow....

I was alone, not in loneliness, but in a healing solitude....

I walked the rocks back to sand, then to the car. Lightness and expanse rested within me. I had gone the distance, as far as I could go at that point in time. Deep calls to deep. Three roses unfolded in an ocean and unfolded me just a little more.

Out of the Ashes: Healing in the Afterloss (Rose Petals on Ash)

Sorrow and loss can either freeze a moment in time or they can become the catalyst for their loving presence touching your life in a deeper and more meaningful way, day after day, year after year. The creation of the Rose Ceremony offered me a sacred place to honor the lives of my wife and two children; and helped me move into a different relationship with what had gone missing and what still remains.

On the anniversaries of their deaths and birthdays, I take a rose to a body of water, the ocean if possible. I release a petal from the rose and hold it close while a specific memory of something we shared surfaces. I say, "Thank you." Then I kiss the petal and release it into the water.

But there is something much more going on. Within the act of kissing the petal and its release with gratitude is the subterranean integration of what is found within the missing, and what unfolds in me that lives in our unfolding for the rest of my life.

The Rose Ceremony symbolizes the reintegration process that goes on throughout our lives. That part of me that went with them into the expanse has forever relocated, and that part of them that stayed with me, and continually unfolds in me, is what is reintegrated into my new relationship with them.

Let me give you an example. As stated from the quote earlier from the book, Matt was my teacher. I am still unpacking all Matt had to teach me in my life, but also, I am learning new things, having new experiences because our connectedness in the expanse expands me here and now.

When someone we love dies our relationship with them does not die. It changes. What was is not gone. Our relationship continues in a different form, in different ways, with a touch of my lips on soft petals, with a memory that comes and with a presence that is always there.

The yearning for connection
is an integral part of life.
The yearning to know, to love
and to connect to another
does not end at death

Benjamin Allen

TheAfterloss.com

Reflection:

Creating your own ritual or ceremony:

For me the rose ceremony emerged in an organic way. There is no 'right' way to do it. It begins with just being present to what needs to emerge, given the relationship you had, the environment you are in, etc. Since I spread their ashes in the sea, water needed to be a part of my ceremony.

So if you feel drawn to create a ceremony of your own, you might want to consider how to include some of the things your loved one enjoyed, or things you used to do together, and incorporate that into your ritual.

Examples could include:

- Sitting in a special place
- Planting seeds
- Lighting candles
- A special piece of music
- Singing special songs
- Preparing certain foods you love
- Writing a letter and then burning it
- Going for a walk and gathering objects you are drawn to (e.g., leaves, pebbles, sea-glass, etc. and making a special arrangement
- Scrap-booking
- Creating an altar and placing special objects on it
- Scattering rose petals

Is there a particular ceremony, or ceremonies, you do to honor your loved one? What is it or are they?

Are there any ceremonies you would like to add?

I will always
feel the presence
of my loved ones,
and doing things
that honor them is
for me a statement
of our ongoing
love.

- Benjamin Allen

TheAfterLoss.com

All those years ago I wanted so desperately to know Matt was okay. I wanted something, anything that would not only signal that he was still on journey, but that we were still on journey. I wanted to know the intertwining of our lives was still unfolding no matter the distance or dimension. That day in Monterey I just wanted a sign that he was okay. As the dolphins passed me I realized the message was more than Matt was okay. I sat on the rock looking over the expanse with the most tender message I could have ever received. The message from Matt was not "I'm okay" but "You're okay."

Out of the Ashes: Healing in the Afterloss (Epilogue)

We need to find a new way of relating to those we love we can no longer physically touch. In the following areas we will explore what works for you. How do you embrace the changes and find ways that are authentic for you in your unfolding relationship with them?

This is not about being stuck in the past. Nor is it about "moving on." This is about moving into a deeper relationship, a different relationship, an ongoing relationship that honors the past, lives fully in the present, and opens to the movement of life that carries the past, present and future in a way that leaves nothing behind, and leaves nothing of this moment behind either. It is about "moving into" a deeper way of life and not forcing an impossibility of "moving on."

So, these exercises are designed to focus on how our physical, emotional, mental and spiritual aspects unfold in the light of this new relationship with those we love. These four guides will take you deeper into the "moving into" the landscape of your Afterloss.

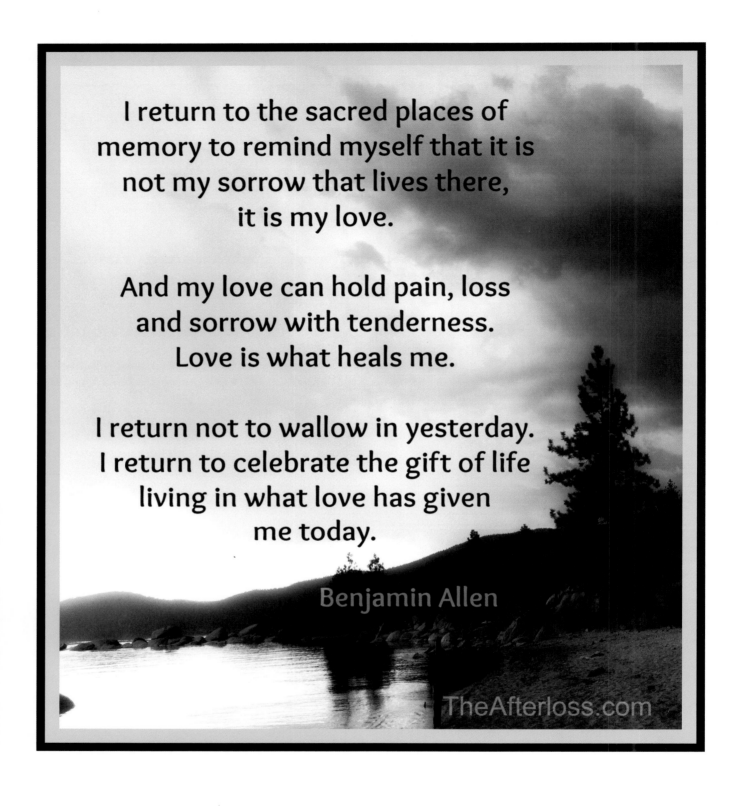

I return to the sacred places of
memory to remind myself that it is
not my sorrow that lives there,
it is my love.

And my love can hold pain, loss
and sorrow with tenderness.
Love is what heals me.

I return not to wallow in yesterday.
I return to celebrate the gift of life
living in what love has given
me today.

Benjamin Allen

TheAfterloss.com

The New Relationship with the Ones We Will Always Love - The Physical

I traveled those weeks in wait going back to the places that gave testament to Lydia and our children. I drove by apartments we rented, the seminary I attended, hospitals where Lydia worked and the hospital where Matt was born. I sat on beaches where Lydia and I spent our hours. I walked through Golden Gate Park, through the botanical gardens, the museums, the memories. There wasn't one place Lydia and I went that I did not go.

Out of the Ashes: Healing in the Afterloss (The Men on the Bridge)

There is a very physical component to nurturing the healing aspects of our relationship with our loved ones. There are places we touch that were touched by the ones we will always love. We are often magnetically drawn to return to those places, sometimes again and again.

Why? Healing calls us there. It is not just to reminisce. For in our remembrance, there is something else happening. While others may think we are trying to hold on to the past we are actually integrating the past into the present. We touch those places of our past in present tense. This is a beautiful part of the reintegration process. It is a process of finding more of what they left us and what of us left with them.

Every time I go across the Golden Gate Bridge, I am drawn into the times I shared with Lydia. But I am also drawn into the present time I live and how Lydia not only shaped my life and love then, but is still shaping my life and love.

We kissed under one of the pylons the night before we moved from San Francisco to Colorado. And every time I pass that pylon today I kiss the memory and the life I have been given today because of that kiss. Today, this kiss has shaped a heart of gratitude that she is a part of all of who I am and that kiss releases me into a thank you. Thank you for being a part of my life then, now and forever more.

Yes, the past draws us, but so does the present…and the future. Mixed in the seasons of sorrow are the beautiful gifts we have been given left by those we love. The emptiness of loss carries the fullness of life – the fullness of life shared and the sharing of life that continues. Because of, not in spite of, being fully with Lydia I am able be fully here with my wife, Rachel. It is not either I love Lydia or I love Rachel. It is not either I am in the past or in the present. As mentioned earlier, I live a both/and life, not an either/or life.

In the following exercises there is an exploration of what those parts are. Explore what parts of you left with them. We all feel a hole within us when someone we dearly love dies. Explore looking at this emptiness as a part of you that travels into the expanse with the one you love. Perhaps it is not missing. Perhaps that part of you has relocated.

There is a way to look at loss as being an expansion. Many speak not only of the incredible pain incurred in loss, but also the greater awareness of love, compassion and service to the world around us because we have endured such tragedy.

This expansion often happens over time. The initial experiences of loss are more of contraction. The pain is so great. The emptiness is so massive. The bewilderment is beyond the scope of understanding. But contraction can give way to expansion as we lean into every facet of our Afterloss and find a new relationship to loss, life and love.

Whether you are at the beginning of your unfolding loss or you have traveled the world of the Afterloss for a long time, there is a need to lean into whatever you are feeling and express from the heart where the heart is right now.

Remember the unconditional essence of three major tributaries of the Afterloss – 1) be honest with yourself, 2) lean into whatever you experience and 3) follow the heart wherever it leads. Whatever you feel, think or do is determined on how you embrace whatever you think, feel or do. Please do it a gentle heart, no matter how broken your heart is.

So, returning to those physical places are not a trip down memory lane. They are the highways to our healing. It does not need to be a clinging to the past. It can be an embrace of a deeper relationship with them, a deeper relationship with ourselves and deeper relationship to life itself.

The following exercises are an exploration of what you can do physically that reflects the relationship with the ones you love. How can you use this physical part of you to find deeper meaning and relationship with those you love? How can you honor both them and you? There are also exercises that will help you uncover ways you can channel your physical experience of loss into healthy avenues that will enhance the expansion of your relationship with the ones you have lost and will always love.

Reflection:

1. Have you ever been drawn to a place where you shared a meal or had a beautiful experience with your loved one? Have you found yourself holding a relic of remembrance – a photograph, a piece of clothing, a birthday card…, and going back in time and being comforted by the moment that once brought you together and has now become a reflection of the pain of what separates you?

If this is true for you, write about your experience and any feelings that came along with it…

Checking in – connect with your body. Bring to mind your loved one and notice what are you experiencing physically in your body right now? It could be a pleasant or uncomfortable... such as a heaviness in your heart or a peaceful rhythmic beat of your heart, for instance.

Notice what emotions you experienced (and experience) when you recall the scene.

a. What does this experience tell you about yourself?

b. What does this experience tell you about your relationship with your loved one?

c. When you visit these places what do you experience as you leave?

d. What other places are drawing you to visit physically, or if that is unavailable to you, in a photograph or precious relic.

2. If you have the ability to go to the places in the three stories from the beginning of this guide, I suggest you use them as your template for this exercise. However, if it is not possible to physically return to the place of the three stories, pick three places where you can physically go. If you cannot get to a physical location, another way to utilize this exercise is to hold an object of deep meaning to you or a photograph from the previous exercise that will help you connect to the physical aspects you experience within yourself.

There are sacred places uniquely designed for healing grief. These places become sacred by shared memories or significant events that reflect a deeper meaning in the Afterloss.

- Benjamin Allen

Healing in the Afterloss - A Personal Pathway through Grief

Place 1: Describe the Memory

Bring in your senses: what did you see? What did you hear? What textures? What flavors and fragrances? All are part of the mosaic of memory.

What part of you has gone with them?

What part of them is now a part of you?

How does this connection with this memory express itself in today?

Place 2: Describe the Memory

Bring in your senses: what did you see? What did you hear? What textures? What flavors and fragrances? All are part of the mosaic of memory.

What part of you has gone with them?

What part of them is now a part of you?

How does this connection with this memory express itself in today?

Place 3: Describe the Memory

Bring in your senses: what did you see? What did you hear? What textures? What flavors and fragrances? All are part of the mosaic of memory.

What part of you has gone with them?

What part of them is now a part of you?

How does this connection with this memory express itself in today?

I am so grateful for the ability to cry.
Every tear that has been shaped by my heart
within the source of my sorrow finds its way
into the source of my healing.

I have ridden every tear wherever it's led me.
What I have found is that each tear always
leads me into the Expanse. Even though my
tears can often hurt, they can always heal.

TheAfterloss.com

Benjamin Allen

The New Relationship with the Ones We Will Always Love - The Emotional

I had witnessed the waxing and waning of loss and knew its signs well. This dynamic of waxing and waning sorrow could happen in a second, a day, month or year, perhaps a lifetime. The brief explosions of pain were far easier. They rose out of nowhere and ambushed me without warning. They were sharp-edged lightning attacks, but they subsided more quickly. And the scars they left healed quicker. I likened the experience to living on a fault line. The small tremors were a release valve. And I would console myself that the "big one," the earthquake that could take me down for good, was kept at bay for another day.

The slow moving expanses of loss were scarier, more ominous in nature. It silently crept along in the back noise of life, slowly eroding from the edges until it made its way to the center. It seized me, not by brute force like the quick bursts, but by attrition.

The most difficult aspect of the slow waxing sorrow was my inability to stop it. I had long learned that anything I resist I become. The more I tried to avoid the pain, the more I was in pain.

Out of the Ashes: Healing in the Afterloss (Time and Distance)

I needed to lean into every fragment of me and of us. A new relationship with those that had died in my life slowly reshaped into a new mosaic. It was not the relationship of the past. Our physical time was done. I would never hold my baby, my first wife or my older child again. I was done and life would always hold a missing piece leaving me living in the undone.

So, it was here in the undone where I found what they left me. It was in my Afterloss where I found where that part of me went with them.

There will always be longing. There will always be love. Today, I look at my hurt in the longing to love them as the adhesive of life. Not only does it hold together this plane of existence and the transcendent realms beyond this breath, but it also magnetizes us into a union that cannot be captured in words.

When I hurt, I lean into the hurt. I follow the hurt. My longing calls me to the special places in my loss where I find the unfolding of our new relationship. And in that place where I am there and they are here, we find a new way to be in our love, to be loved and to be love.

Do not fear the hurt. When I touch the hurt with unconditional tenderness it transforms into an unconditional transcendent love. Lean into whatever you are going through for it is the best way to get through it.

And it is not just to get through the moment, even though there were times that was all I could do. Leaning into the hurt also is designed to get through the barriers of past, present and future. It is the passageway between and beyond this time and space. The hurt is the ultimate labyrinth leading to an expansive state where love expands our relationship with the ones we will always love and how that love is fluidly reshaping us day by day.

The following exercises are designed to touch those places that hurt. Some will say don't go there, but you are already there. Some will say just get over it, but I say to you go deeper into where the hurt is taking you. We cannot avoid the unavoidable. Loss is the greatest hurt I've ever experienced. Separation singed every fiber of my being. So, I went into the separation and found nothing is separate. Nothing lives in isolation. And the love I live with the ones I will always love awaits me there. And the hurt itself shape shifted and dissolved into healing.

Again, please be gentle with yourself in the following exercises. Do only what you can do. There is no right or wrong, no finish line at the end of this exercise. One layer will lead to the next layer. I have found that one hurt may unfold a multitude of hurts that may be perpetually unfolding me for a long, long time…maybe a lifetime. But each time I unfold another part of me, I find I am in a state of blossoming into the true nature of life, death, loss and love … into healing.

Still, I know the pace and the rhythm of my loss. When I get to a point where I need rest, I rest. Sometimes the exploration of my hurt is in centimeters and seconds. Other times I venture inward in inches and moments. I let love dictate my pace and life dictate my rhythm.

Be aware you are going into the belly of the beast called separation and that in and of itself hurts. But also know separation is only a shadow. When love illumines the dark nature of loss, shadows dissolve into the brilliant nature of love itself. Still, go gently into that good night as it leads to the light of day.

The following exercises are a small sample of how to process the hurt. There are a multitude of hurts that come with loss and a multitude of ways to process it all. However, the following exercises are designed to go deep into just a few. I would encourage you to explore how this process can be used or adapted to your particular experience in your Afterloss. Everyone grieves differently and heals differently. Always follow the beat of your own heart.

Reflections:

1. Name five situations where you are currently experiencing the most hurt, discomfort or pain. (For example – Driving past the theater where Matt and I went for our last movie.)

2. For each of these experiences, get present to the feelings and memories that emerge, and then write about them in a stream of consciousness. Don't think about what you are writing. Whatever shows up write it down and don't stop until you have at least one page. It could be longer, but let whatever you feel come out for at least one page.

3. In each of the five experiences you have chosen, write down in one or two sentences what the theme of your one page of stream of consciousness writing was. (For example – missing our experiencing of sharing movies and feeling the deterioration of our time together. The brevity of life, etc.)

4. For each one, in what way can this new awareness deepen your relationship with the one you have lost? (For example - Opening up to celebrating that Matt and I had that time and that our relationship continues… it wasn't goodbye… still feel his presence when I go to theater or watch a movie we once physically shared together.)

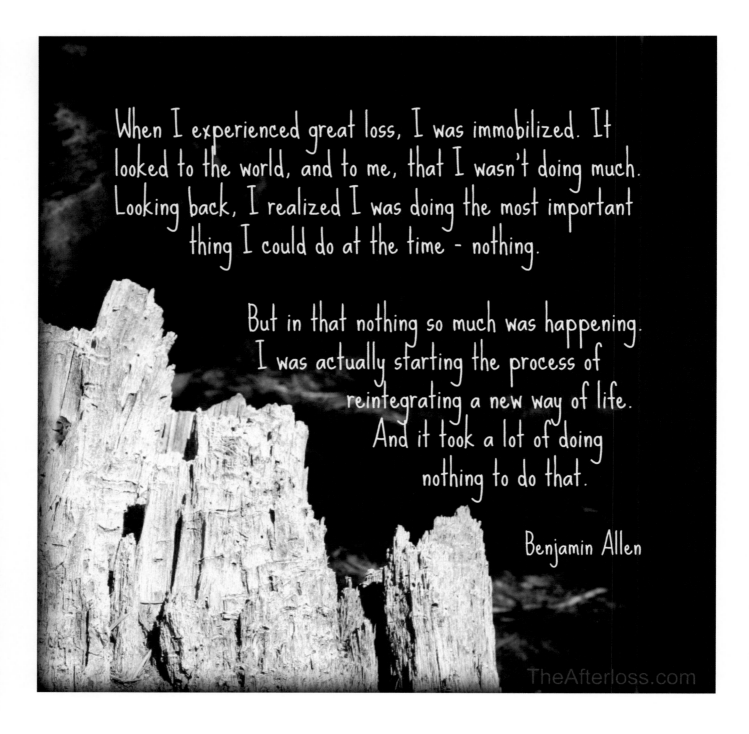

When I experienced great loss, I was immobilized. It looked to the world, and to me, that I wasn't doing much. Looking back, I realized I was doing the most important thing I could do at the time - nothing.

But in that nothing so much was happening. I was actually starting the process of reintegrating a new way of life. And it took a lot of doing nothing to do that.

Benjamin Allen

TheAfterloss.com

The New Relationship with the Ones We Will Always Love - The Mental

I was released from the gravitational pull to a belief that wasn't mine.... I no longer lived in negation, no longer measured my peace, my anger, my forgiveness by a God of judgment. I was free to love again. I walked out of the church free to follow my path without living in relation to anything but love – that place beyond beginnings and endings.

Out of the Ashes: Healing in the Afterloss (Now It Is Time to Remember)

Are we still connected to the ones we love and can never physically touch again? Is there a different kind of touch that takes place from the moment of loss into a life of loss? What continues? Does that relationship continue to grow in spite of the physical separation?

The heart can answer these questions, but it is the mind that translates what we believe ends and begins, begins and ends. It is the mind that believes, that filters belief and that guides the manifestation of belief. So, what do you believe?

Belief is as individual as grief. This guidebook is not about creating a belief. It is about helping you understand what you believe and how you wish to live in that belief.

I'm sure you can tell by now that my personal belief is my relationship with those I can no longer physically touch continues to grow and unfold. My relationship with my sons, Matt and Bryan, did not end upon Matt's death at the age of 13 or Bryan's death at the age of 8 and half months. When they took that part of me into the expanse I continued to grow in the expanse. When a part of them stayed with me we continue to grow within this lifetime. I do not relate today with Matt as a 13 year old or Bryan as an infant. I have grown and we have grown into a relationship beyond the width of time and within the depths of time.

My mind was drawn to this perception of our ongoing relationship and the ever-unfolding nature of love in both the infinite of the expanse and the finite of this time and space. I have felt life's being out of sync with what was Before and what is and my mind has interpreted that as love stretching me across the universe. I am here. I am there. We are here. We are there.

This may or may not resonate with you. What is important is what does resonate with you. What is authentic for you? What do you believe? Does this belief align with the heart, with spirit, and with the loss that is unfolding you?

The following questions offer an opportunity to examine your beliefs and what you think. Thought is a very powerful expression. What you think can either illumine or darken the pathways of your Afterloss. My belief is that the darkness is derived from adopting someone else's belief that is not truly aligned to yours. And the illumination comes from within your true, authentic self shining from what you truly believe. Whatever you believe, please give yourself permission to step on the solid foundation of that belief and let it shine the pathways of your Afterloss.

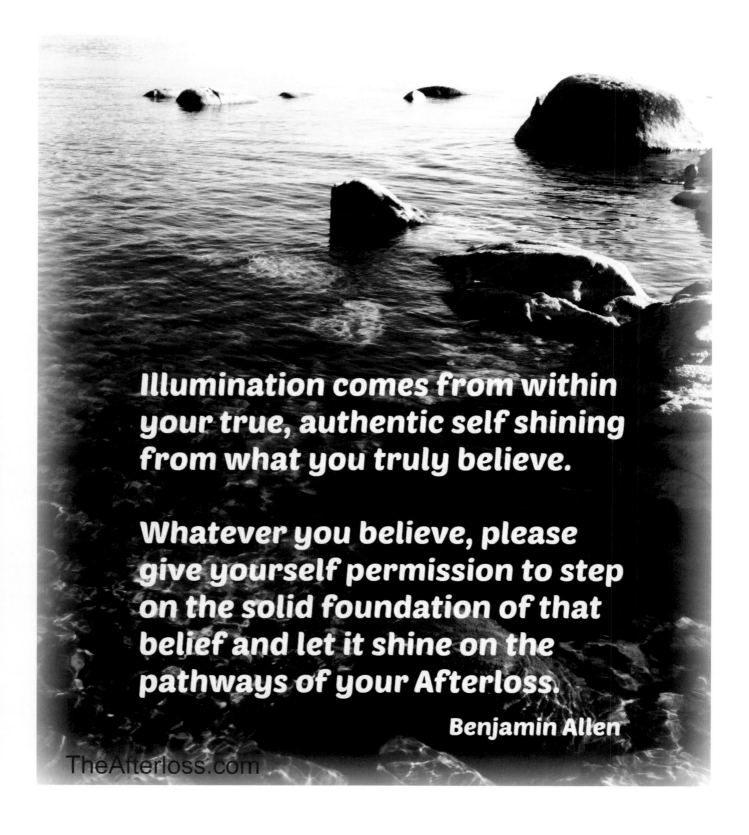

Illumination comes from within your true, authentic self shining from what you truly believe.

Whatever you believe, please give yourself permission to step on the solid foundation of that belief and let it shine on the pathways of your Afterloss.

Benjamin Allen

TheAfterloss.com

Reflection:

Do you believe we are still connected to the ones we love and can never physically touch again or not? What is your belief and experience?

Is there a different kind of touch that takes place from the moment of loss into a life of loss?

What continues for you?

Does that relationship continue to grow in spite of the physical separation? What is your experience?

To find freedom, I needed to find forgiveness. To find healing, I needed to come to a place where I forgave everything, including me. Today, I have no regrets, but it has been an arduous journey to find freedom and healing, to live in forgiveness.

Benjamin Allen

The New Relationship with the Ones We Will Always Love - The Spiritual

I discovered a freedom was on offer in each moment, embedded in the small seconds of every breath, layered in the body that carried me.

The large questions of life that weighed so heavily on me began to lift. I had been looking in the wrong direction. It was just a beginning, and quite often painful. Freedom is not all it's cracked up to be.

Freedom confronted me with what wasn't free within me.

Out of the Ashes: Healing in the Afterloss (The Same Life)

Spirit, the meaning within spirit and how we touch that part of us in relation to our loved ones, is the act of connection. Spirit is the DNA of essence and essence is the pulsating lifeblood of our physical, emotional and mental being. For those who have a religious tradition that articulates spirit, there are ways to express that connection with those who have died before us. For those that have a belief in the transcendent nature of life, but are not part of a particular religious expression, there are also ways to connect life and death. And for those who are using this guide that do not believe there is anything beyond death, there are ways to connect and honor the life of the ones we love and can no longer touch, too.

What blocks us from experiencing the fullness of life and meaning, even in the midst of loss? Here is an opportunity to focus on any obstacles in the way of your relating to the ones you will always love.

Pain is not an obstacle to connection. The resistance to the pain blocks us from moving forward into deeper relationships with the ones we love that have died and the ones we love we can still touch.

The barriers I created are what I came to see as my protective layers. I hurt so bad. I had so much anger. I lived in terror more than fear for when the day would come when one of them would die. I had no idea where the magnitude of my aloneness would lead me in my state of sorrowed anguish. I just wanted to push the world away. It like was pounding my hand with a hammer and then squeezing the hand to deal with the pain.

So, in order to survive I built these protective layers. I had been hurt beyond belief and I was determined not to be hurt again and again and again.

But these weren't protective layers. They were prisons. I had imprisoned myself within my pain, my hurt, my anger, my fear…my aloneness.

When the pain became unbearable I had to find a way to escape the prisons I had created. I had to lean into everything that blocked me from living free. Gratefully, the prison I had locked myself into had a key to the door. But,this key worked on the inside of the door, not the outside. My way out was to go all the way inside and open the door to life again and be set free.

The following exercise is a tremendous challenge. It is not easy to look at what blocks us from living in connection with life. As I have encouraged you to do in the past, please be gentle with yourself. Touch these protective layers without judgment. Hold the tender, painful parts of you with unconditional care. The pain is not there to hurt you. The pain is crying out to heal you.

What I had to do was to lean into every physical, emotional, mental and spiritual parts of my pain. I had to honestly look at what blocked me from living and go wherever it took me. I needed to follow every tributary of loss and pain in my Afterloss to its end in order to begin releasing the protective layers that imprisoned me.

Ultimately, this relentless pursuit of peace brought me to peace, brought me to a place of peace within the pain. I will always carry pain in some form or another, but I carry it differently. I carry it in peace.

Please do the following exercises with self-care. This isn't about forcing yourself to battle through whatever is blocking you. It is about gently holding the protective layer and letting the sunlight of the spirit of your honesty and sincerity melt the barriers away. Be who you are and where you are unconditionally.

If there are places you cannot go yet, don't go. It is not time yet and there is no way to force peace. You don't need to find spirit. If you are open, spirit will find you, whatever spirit means to you.

And if you are open to peace, peace will find you, wherever you are. It is there peace will embrace you and you will be able to unlock that layer from the inside, layer after layer, into a state of freedom. Let the gentle embrace of the pain in your multi-layered landscape of the Afterloss be your pathway to freedom. Let the dissolving of your protective layers be one of the keys that set you free.

The following exercises are to see what is blocking you from experiencing life to its fullest. It is an opportunity to let go of unfinished business, to find forgiveness and self-forgiveness, to release anything that is holding you back from holding the ones you love in a new way.

Reflection: **Unfinished Business**

Is there any unfinished business between you and your loved one? Or is there something you'd like to say to them right now? Perhaps there is something you wish to thank them for or something you wish to tell them. It can be anything, but here you can tell them everything, everything you want to, anything you need to express.

If there is anything you want to express, get a notebook and pen, find a time when you won't be disturbed and bring yourself to a quiet place. Sit quietly, connect with your authentic self and connect in your heart with the person. Feel into what you wish to say. And then write. Allow the words to flow, without judgment. Take your time and let the letter unfold in its own way.

When you're done, choose what you wish to do with the letter. You might want to read it out loud in a special place, or read it to a safe person. You may want to release it into flames that return it all to ash. Think of what works best for you and go with what honors both you and your loved one.

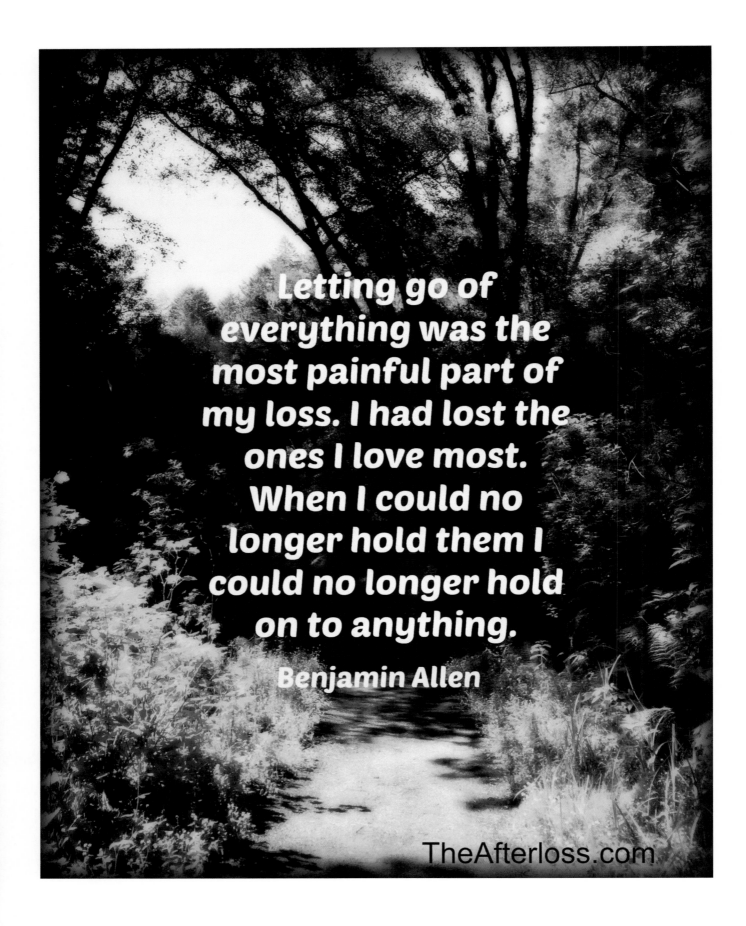

Letting go of everything was the most painful part of my loss. I had lost the ones I love most. When I could no longer hold them I could no longer hold on to anything.

Benjamin Allen

TheAfterloss.com

Reflection: **Forgiveness**

Do you feel the need to forgive anyone?

On a separate piece of paper, ask God, Spirit or your higher consciousness (whatever is aligned to your belief system) to show you anyone you need to forgive that is blocking you from your peace.

In a stream of consciousness, list every person that comes to mind whether it makes sense or not. Do not filter or edit the list.

Then, by their name write specifically what you believe they did (could be multiple events and write each one) that is blocking you from your peace.

Then, take each name and each event and say, " I forgive you. I bless you and release you to your highest good. And please bless me and release me to my highest good." Even if you don't mean it, do this every day for a week and see if you experience a releasing from the blockage and a new freedom. If you feel a release, continue to do this every day until you find the freedom of forgiveness.

After a week of following the previous suggestion, next to each name and each event write what it will take to let go completely into forgiveness. Do you need to talk to them and clear the air? Do you need to do something else to be released from this blockage to your peace?

When you feel you have found the blockages removed, then have a ceremony to celebrate your release. Perhaps light a candle and let the flame burn the list of what once held you captive into what now has set you free.

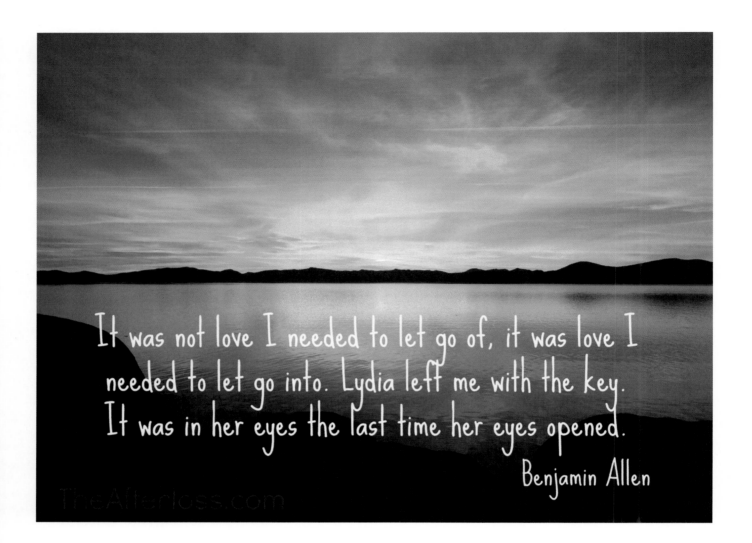

It was not love I needed to let go of, it was love I needed to let go into. Lydia left me with the key. It was in her eyes the last time her eyes opened.

Benjamin Allen

TheAfterloss.com

Reflection: **Self-Forgiveness**

Ask God, Spirit or your higher consciousness (whatever is aligned to your belief system) to show you anything you are carrying that you are unable to forgive yourself for that is blocking you from your peace.

On a separate piece of paper, in a stream of consciousness, write the specific events that come to mind without censoring or editing.

Then, take each event and say, "Forgive me. And bless and release me to my highest good. And I forgive me for I am release to live in my highest good."

Read the list every day for a week and speak this act of forgiveness. Even if you don't mean it, this simple act can have very interesting results. If you feel after a week of practicing self-forgiveness there is a shift, continue until you feel this blockage to your peace has been set free.

When you feel you have found the blockages removed, then have a ceremony to celebrate your release. Perhaps light a candle and let the flame burn the list of what once held you captive into what now has set you free.

We are not the same, and neither is our world. How we relate to others is part of the landscape of the Afterloss and unfolding of life.

Benjamin Allen

A New Relationship with the World We Live in Now

We enter places where we think we are totally alone, where no one can possibly understand, only to discover the paths we walk have so many previous footprints. We are not as alone as we may think. Someone has traveled this path before. What did they find? What am I finding as we share the brevity of our heartbeat and the timelessness of our questions?

Out of the Ashes: Healing in the Afterloss (Introduction)

The initial impact of loss is that of separation, becoming separate from the one or ones we dearly love. There is a tremendous aloneness in loss. Many feel that no one could ever possibly know how they feel and what they are going through; and to a certain degree they are right. There is a uniqueness to grief, just as there is a uniqueness to each one of us.

On the other hand, there is universality to loss. No one escapes beginnings or endings whether it is the death of a loved one, the death of dream or any other death. Birth and death are a part of each one of us. So, we may not know specifically what someone is going through in their loss, but we know what we are going through and as we touch our own pain we arrive at the collective experience of loss in the world around us.

This is a section of the guidebook where we will examine what is happening within the re-integration process we are experiencing with the world we live in now. We are not the same and neither is our world. How we relate to others is part of the landscape of our Afterloss and unfolding of life. We emerge from our world of the Afterloss and it takes effort and intentionality to find the connecting points with this new world. Ultimately, the two worlds can find a harmonic resonance that honors both loss and life.

However, the world of Before is gone for us, but not for many of the ones around us. Many of our friends and love ones momentarily pause and then return to their normal rhythm and pace. They are the ones that go on while we are the ones that go in; and in our Afterloss, it is a different rhythm and a different pace.

As mentioned earlier, often people in great loss are told they need to "move on." This implies leaving something or someone behind. We "continue on" in life, but we will carry loss the rest of our life.

We do not live solely in the Afterloss. That world that buzzes around us is a world that needs to be blended with that world that moves within us.

We do not need to give up our love, our memories and our ongoing relationship with our loved ones to continue life in the world around us. It is not an either/or paradigm. True healing is living in a both/and world.

The following exercises focus on how the rhythm and pace of the Afterloss has affected you in the light of in the world around you. How do you find a meeting point in two worlds that are often experienced as out of sync? Where does the world within you surface in the world around you? And how can you live in both without doing damage to either?

Not surprisingly, how we relate to the world with live in now involves our physical, emotional, mental and spiritual selves. These aspects of us greatly affect the world around us. And also, their relationship with the world give us clues as to how we are doing in living in our loss.

When the world of the Afterloss and the World Out There meet, stress can arise. Stress over little things, small tasks, things that used to be so simple.

I liken it to pole vaulting over anthills. I have come to realize it is the task within me that has me incapacitated, not the tasks Out There.

Benjamin Allen

TheAfterloss.com

The New Relationship with the World We Live in Now - The Physical

I liked going down to San Francisco during anniversary times for three reasons. First, the beauty of nature that lies in pockets of the city, where Lydia and I took refuge on many days, helped me touch memory. Second, Half Moon Bay, the burial waters, drew me to her shore for the rose ceremony. And third, coffee shops on densely populated streets gave energy to the weariness that loss took.

I watched people with hurried lives hurry by. It was pure voyeurism. But it had purpose. The days before the day of the rose ceremony I slowed. Grief drained most of the emotional and spiritual resources I had. Coffee shops reminded me that I was the one off kilter. The world was still turning with normal people living normal lives.

Out of the Ashes: Healing in the Afterloss (Rose Petals on Ash)

When we find ourselves submerged into the Afterloss, we experience time differently. The world around us that is living in the world of Before goes at a different pace. Many times this feeling of being out of sync is interpreted as something is wrong. But nothing is wrong. It is simply different.

There is a different rhythm and pace to loss, especially in the beginning, but in my experience it is simply part of the landscape of my life even today. It is not as intense as it was in the beginning. And my world today has found a blended harmony with my Afterloss and the world in which I live. Nevertheless, the subtle difference between those that have not experience such loss leaves me on one level or another out of sync, even if it is ever so slightly.

Some need to be with others as the devastation of loss unfolds. Still others who are sifting through all the changes loss brings need time alone. There is no one way that is the best way to show up for the world around us. The most important part of being in the world you live in now is being true to yourself.

It is important to know the rhythm of your own grief. Trying to force yourself to be with others when that is not where you want to be is not helpful and neither is being alone when you feel you need to be out in the world with someone, or doing some activity.

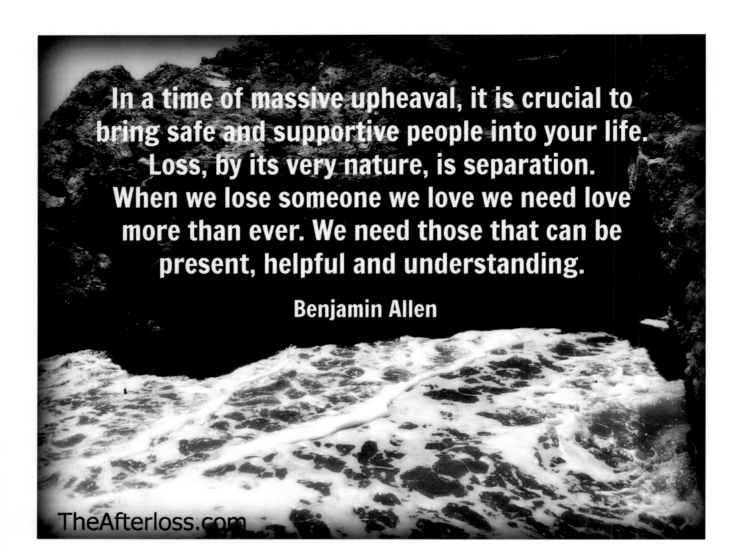

In a time of massive upheaval, it is crucial to bring safe and supportive people into your life. Loss, by its very nature, is separation. When we lose someone we love we need love more than ever. We need those that can be present, helpful and understanding.

Benjamin Allen

TheAfterloss.com

Reflection:
How do you grieve in relation to the world around you?

When do you need to be alone?

When is it helpful to be with others?

What activities do you feel are helpful to you?

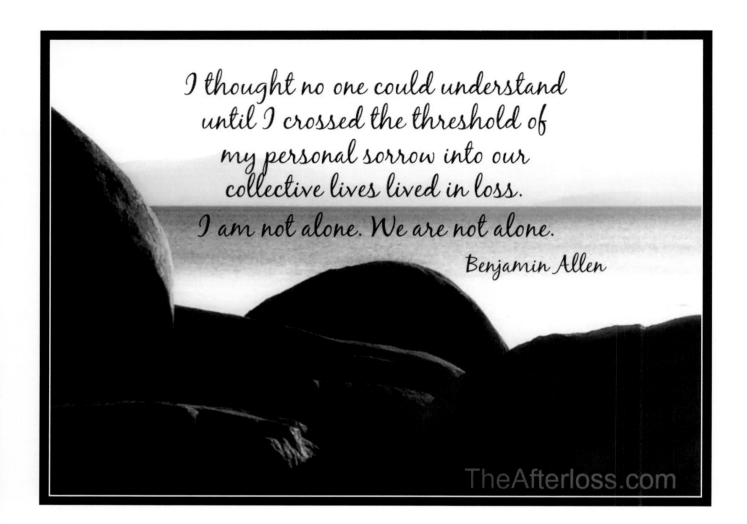

I thought no one could understand
until I crossed the threshold of
my personal sorrow into our
collective lives lived in loss.
I am not alone. We are not alone.

Benjamin Allen

TheAfterloss.com

The New Relationship with the World We Live in Now - The Emotional

But the grief process confused me, kept me off balance as it pressed against my daily life. I had a tremendous difficulty in discerning what I felt, the origin of the feeling, beginnings and endings of a thought, a feeling, and a moment....
I felt like I was hanging onto a tree in a hurricane. The bark of the tree tore my skin, but I couldn't let go. The gale force winds hurled heavy objects into me, but I couldn't let go. I held tighter as each thought, each event, each moment perpetually bashed me between the hurricane and the tree. Every day I just hung on for dear life.

Then the eye of the hurricane passed over me. And there was my moment of truth. I could either let go of the tree and follow the stillness of the eye, or hold on as the stillness moved on and the torrential winds tore at me again. It would appear on the surface to be a no brainer, but hurricanes were what I knew best. Stillness was a foreign commodity to me.

Out of the Ashes: Healing in the Afterloss (The Eye of the Hurricane)

Safe People

Where do you feel safe to feel? When we are in intense grief we need an outlet. We need safe places and safe people. Sadly, not all of those around us are safe, even some of our closest family or friends.

In most cases, it is not because they don't care or don't want to be there. It's because they can't. They have their own sorrow, and everyone deals with sorrow differently. Another reason why some people we think will be there aren't is because they are not in the same kind of intensity as us. How could my dear friend who has no children ever feel the loss of my child like I did?

What I learned was to accept people where they were at, where they could be there for me and where they could not. I dropped my expectations. Everybody is just doing the best they can to cope with their own loss in their own emotional survival under such tragic circumstances. The emotional upheavals affect everyone touched by the one we can no longer touch to one degree or another, but the way they deal with their loss will not be the same as the way I deal with my loss.

However, it is still important to find those that can be there for you. Finding someone that doesn't try to fix the sorrow, or divert the pain gives us the conduit to feel what we need to feel. Having someone in your life that doesn't judge you for how you need to express your emotions is a beautiful gift. Sitting with someone who holds your shattered heart while you pick up piece by piece and feel what it feels to be shattered is one of the most beautiful acts of love we can ever experience in a time when we are separated from all that was and grasping for anything that is left. Find those safe people that can do this. Reach out as you reach in.

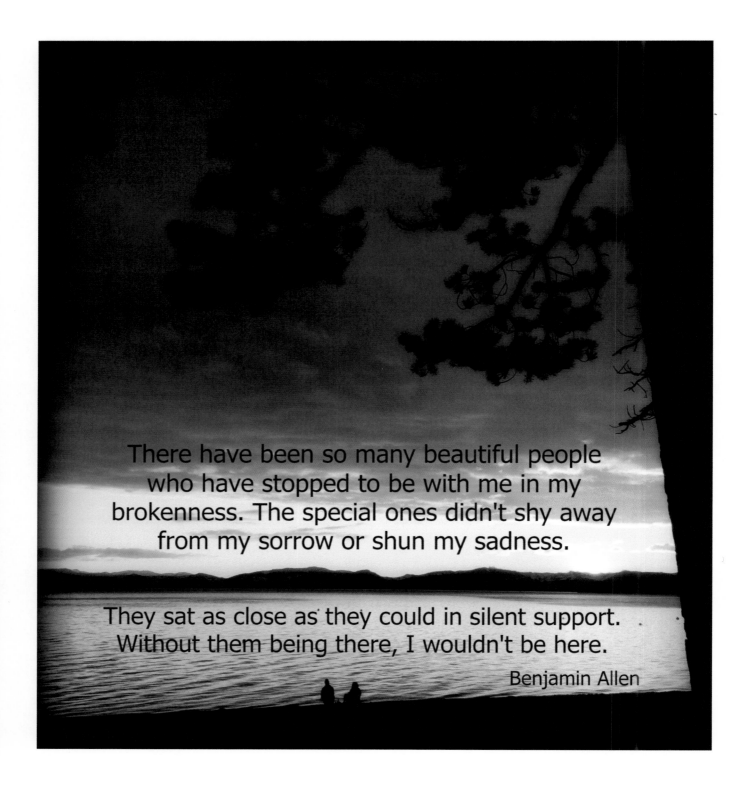

There have been so many beautiful people who have stopped to be with me in my brokenness. The special ones didn't shy away from my sorrow or shun my sadness.

They sat as close as they could in silent support. Without them being there, I wouldn't be here.

Benjamin Allen

Reflection:
Where are your places of peace?

Who are safe people with whom you can just be you? Where is the eye of your hurricane?

When someone says, "I know how you feel," we know instinctively whether they are just words or they truly know how we feel.

We know if they are trying to fill an awkward silence or they are coming from a place where only silence can speak.

Benjamin Allen

Reflection:

Write about the following questions:

What expectations of others do you have for being there for you? Are they realistic?

How do you respond when someone says something insensitive?

How do you feel when others show up for you?

How do you feel when others don't show up for you?

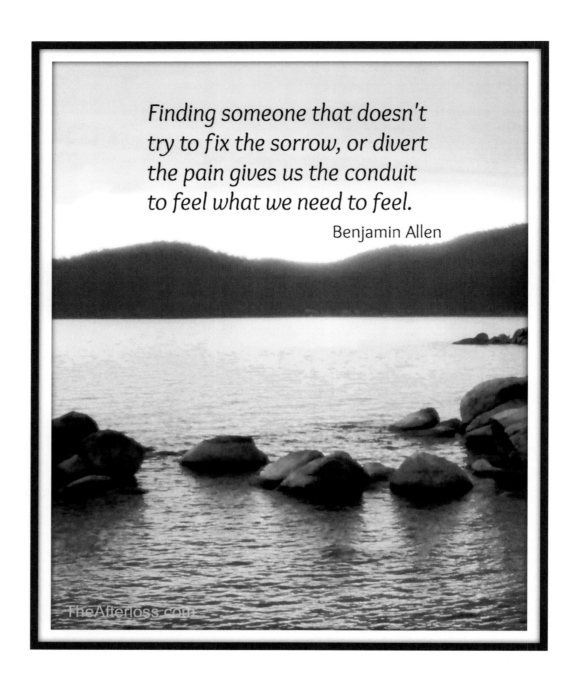

Finding someone that doesn't try to fix the sorrow, or divert the pain gives us the conduit to feel what we need to feel.

Benjamin Allen

TheAfterloss.com

Make a list of people you can trust to be present for you unconditionally.

Is there someone with whom you can check in daily or at least weekly?

Are there people you can call on for specific support (e.g., help with shopping? Driving you somewhere? etc.)

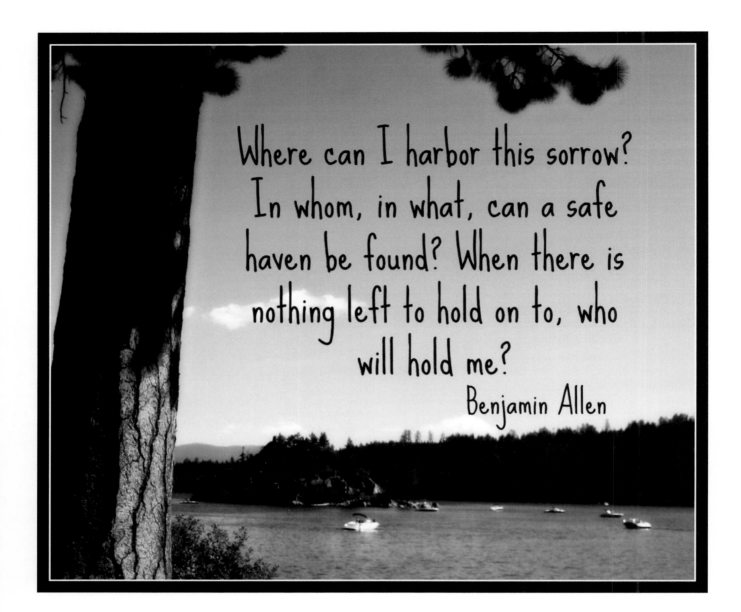

Where can I harbor this sorrow? In whom, in what, can a safe haven be found? When there is nothing left to hold on to, who will hold me?

Benjamin Allen

Safe Places

The moment of loss does not stop time; the moment of loss expands time. The timeless nature of loss stretches us across the universe, beyond the world in which we walk and breathe. In that reintegration process of unfolding what part of us went with them and what part of them stayed with us, there is a need to take time in the timelessness of grief to unfold this new relationship with ourselves, with them and with the world around us. And this takes a safe place to do it.

Not every place we go in a day is a safe place to feel the magnitude of our emotional upheaval. There are times we have to suspend sorrow and try to blend our Afterloss into the world of Before. Life goes on for the world around us. But for us, life goes in. Life goes in the realms of the Afterloss that take us to the depths of our being. This can't be done everywhere or at anytime. It needs to be a safe place to be in order for us to be so open and vulnerable in our emotional fluidity.

It is not about hiding your emotions. It is about suspending their expression *until* you are in a safe place. Such a place is a sacred place. It is where the fluidity of our sorrow can flow freely from a river of tears into the ocean's expanse. Find your sacred places that hold you as you let go of all that you feel into all that can be felt.

Find nurturing places you can feel the full depths of your Afterloss and lean into the reintegration process. Where can you just let go into everything you feel? There is a balance.

Reflection:

Where do you feel emotionally safe?

How can you hold your feelings when it is not appropriate or safe to let them flow into the world around you?

What activities are emotionally healing for you?

The gift my Afterloss has given me is the permission to ask anything unconditionally without retribution. If I am to find peace, I must exclude nothing, embrace everything and accept, at the deepest level, what I find.

Benjamin Allen

TheAfterloss.com

The New Relationship with the World We Live in Now – The Mental

I wondered if there was anything left in me to use. In my unfolding it was a tenuous time. I didn't know what was truly left. It would be a large leap for me to enter the world again.

I traveled down to San Francisco and sat next to busy streets wondering if I could live there again, if there was a place for me in hard-soled shoes on concrete. Where did I belong? I truly questioned if I could ever rejoin the human race again. The thought frightened me and it cut both ways. I feared I would never resurface again and I was afraid I just might.

Out of the Ashes: Healing in the Afterloss (Glass Beach, Glass Steps)

One of the hardest things to understand is how the world around us keeps moving at such a pace when the world within us has fallen into the Afterloss's time warp. I felt like I was moving in slow motion as the world buzzed by when loss first happened. And there are times even today when I feel out of sync with priorities and focuses that others have.

Matt was three when his little brother, Bryan, died. Lydia was very sick at the time and there were no treatments yet for HIV. We lived day by day in the loss of our child, in the losing of Lydia and in the fear of ultimately losing Matt. It was in the midst of all this that I thought, "Tomorrow was a long time ago."

The future dissolved into today. Time playing with Matt on the playground superseded saving for his college education. Building a career didn't matter. Retirement plans were senseless. Everything was re-prioritized into what was important now. Loss took my future, but gave me a richness only the present can give. I learned what this moment, and every moment, truly means.

So, now when I reflect on how tomorrow was such a long time ago, I am no longer in resignation of a future lost. I embrace the illusion of tomorrow in the sunlight of today.

Everyone has their own pathway through their Afterloss and find what is important to them. What I have found is that moments are more important than hours and today is more important than tomorrow. Lydia, Matt and Bryan taught me how precious today is. My priority is to live this day in honor of the lesson they taught me. I have found that the best way to prepare for tomorrow is to live fully in *this* day.

The quality of my life is a precious commodity. Being with those I love, doing what I love and being of love have a greater emphasis in my life. It is not what I have that has meaning now. It is what I have to give that fills me.

The Afterloss beckons the world of Before to make an account of itself. What the world around us finds as important may or may not be important now. The mental constructs that went unquestioned are questioned.

Deeper questions from the depths of our loss deepen us. Is this what I really want to be doing with my life? Is spending time here the best use of both my time and my here? What do I really want to do with my life? And the ultimate question – What can I give to the world around me and to life?

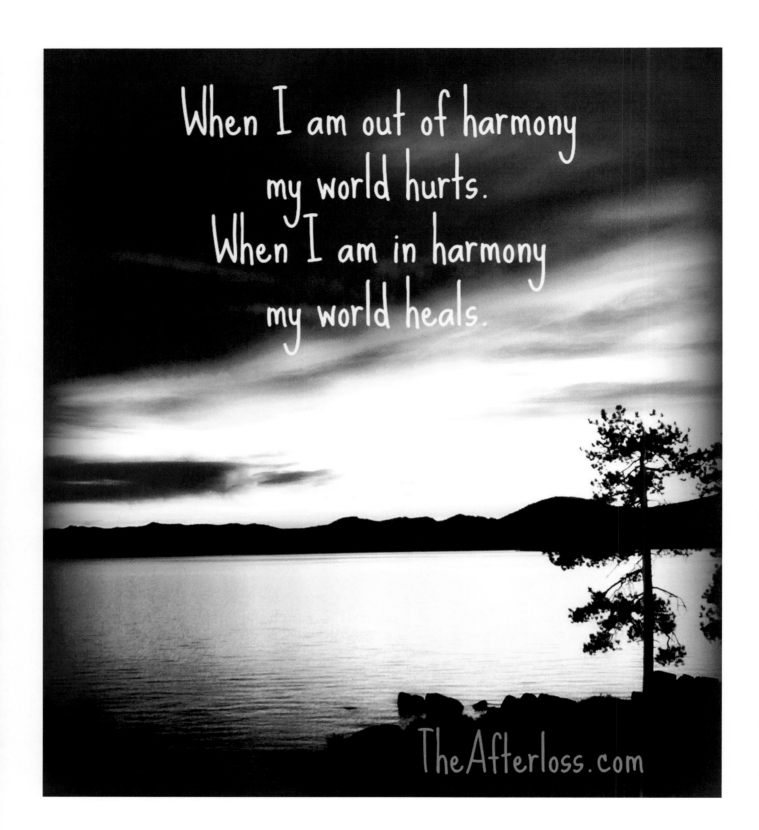

When I am out of harmony
my world hurts.
When I am in harmony
my world heals.

TheAfterloss.com

Reflection:

Are you doing what you want to do today?

What is important for you now that you are experiencing living with loss?

In a stream of consciousness, list all the priorities in your life.

With the list of priorities, arrange them in the order of importance.

My one request is that my sorrow can be the salve to help heal, not just me, but us. And that we can become the healer of wounds.

Benjamin Allen

The New Relationship with the World We Live in Now – The Spiritual

A year and a half in Mendocino began to change me. I sat on Glass Beach with a future. I had not had one in such a long time. It felt strange, frightening. I had lived longer than my past could hold me, but I did not know if the future was a sustainable option.

Observing the ebb and flow of grief was still my meaning, but it was time for me to leave Mendocino. If I had stayed I would have created a shrine to my family and hidden under the sprawling stars and ocean sunsets. As appealing as that might have been, it would have been the end of me. True stillness resides in motion.

Out of the Ashes: Healing in the Afterloss (Glass Beach, Glass Steps)

This new relationship with life, born out of loss, unfolds from within our Afterloss into the world we are still living. The challenge in the "continuing on" is how you tap into this transcendent source and how you translate it into your daily life. As mentioned before, however you translate meaning, whether it is God, Spirit or some other name or concept that attempts to describe the indescribable, the question becomes how does meaning manifest in your life right here and right now?

As mentioned in the previous section, what I believe to be the most important question I face in both life and loss is what can I give to life? How can I be of service to the world around me?

There are so many that have been touched by loss that have ultimately come to the place of service out of that loss. Whatever belief system you embrace and how you articulate what you believe, there is a place for the transformation of tragedy into the transcendence of life within loss.

I did not write *Out of the Ashes: Healing in the Afterloss* for me. I had already found my pathway into a rhythm and rhyme of healing for me when I decided to write my story. I live now in the perpetual unfolding of the expanse of my loss, life and love. I wrote the book for those that venture the same path of loss in their own way and may find my experiences helpful with healing in the Afterloss.

I truly believe coming to a place of service is the greatest blossoming of the reintegration process of grief. What our loved ones leave us is so often translated into how we can give back to life. This meaning can motivate and transform into what I can give the world I live in now. The ones I love empower me to reach within and beyond my sorrow into a greater context of a life of service. I give because I have been given so much.

The following exercises are designed to help you unpack what you believe and how you want to live this belief in the world around you.

To live life to the fullest is a testament to their lives and all they mean to me.

Benjamin Allen

Reflection:

What can you give back to yourself?

What can you give to the ones you love and will always love?

What can you give to the world you live in now?

Closure is defined as
finality. But for me, there
is nothing final in loss.
Life does not begin with
birth and does not end
with death. Every
season...everyone...every
moment closes into an
opening.

Benjamin Allen

TheAfterloss.com

Conclusion

Nothing in the universe is wasted. Spirit became flesh. What was the body to teach me? What gifts lay within skin and bones, the anatomy of Spirit? Somewhere in the interchange of heaven and earth I lived through Spirit, through illusion, in a body, within the dream.

I can see this dream as a horrible nightmare or a dream filled with beauty and love. I can embrace this dream as a blessing or a curse. Either way it is the same dream.

In the final analysis this is my dream. And what a wonderful dream it is. It is a dream beyond beginnings and endings, without a start or finish. It is the intricate dance of the physical, emotional and spiritual structures that unfold the mystery of me.

Matt was right. "The meaning of life is life itself."

Out of the Ashes: Healing in the Afterloss (It's Just a Dream)

The ultimate meaning of your loss is yours and yours alone. No one can completely understand what your loved one meant to you, and means to you now. There is a part of loss that is indescribable. There are no words. It is in the deepest realms of our Afterloss where we discover our deepest meaning.

This meaning comes from all of who we are, what we believe… and what gives meaning. It comes out of the blue, like a blue sky glistening in the morning light. It comes out of our deepest darkness, like a moonless night sky canopied over a barren desert. It comes from the world within us and settles within the ever-changing moment in the world around us.

Meaning unfolds. It unfolds what is important to us. It unfolds the treasures of our time with them and the invaluable moments that now are an integral part of the landscape in every moment.

Loss is unfolding as well. Love for the ones who have died does not die. The unfolding of our dance together continues within a different embrace, a different tune… and a different meaning. What once was so important can become meaningless. As our meaning unfolds, we discover a deeper experience of life, loss and love.

We are forever changed by loss. The question is how do we choose to change? What do we keep? What do we let go of? Where do we go from here? What is left of us and what is left for us? What now?
The answers to all these questions, and more, are tributaries that flow from the greatest question of all –
What is the meaning of life, loss and love? More importantly, what does life, loss and love mean to you?

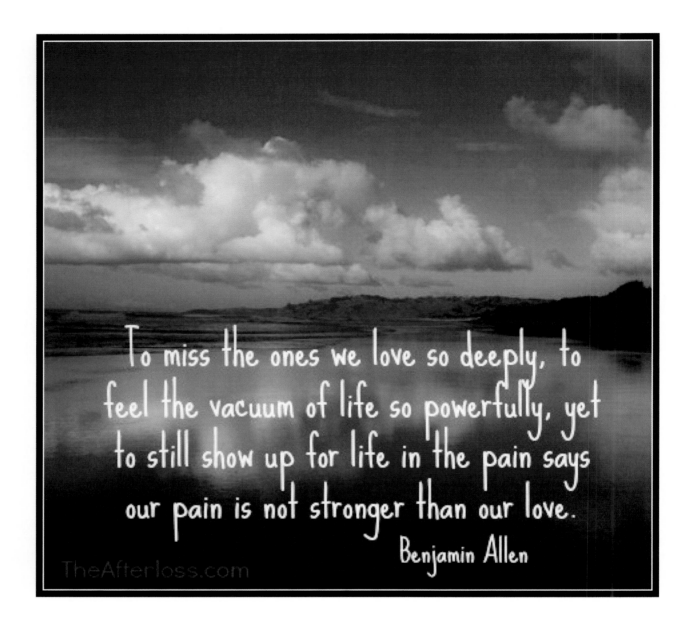

To miss the ones we love so deeply, to feel the vacuum of life so powerfully, yet to still show up for life in the pain says our pain is not stronger than our love.

Benjamin Allen

TheAfterloss.com

Reflection:

Revisit the three stories you chose at the beginning of this workbook. Think about how each one of these precious memories is important to you. In each one, write about what the meaning behind the story is for you and how this can heal you.

Story 1 _____

Story 2 _____

Story 3 _____

*I thought this pain
would last forever.*

*Gratefully I was
wrong.*

*It is the love that is
lasting forever.*

Benjamin Allen

A Letter of Love

Thank you. Thank you for giving me the privilege of walking this path with you. Thank for being willing to lean into your loss and let it take you wherever it led, and hopefully will lead.

My hope is that this process has given you hope…and a way to express your meaning. Just as this is not the beginning of your loss, it is not the end of the journey either. There will be more. If we embrace our loss, life and love, there will always be more.

Hopefully, our time together has been an oasis in your Afterloss, a place where you can stop and rest next to the deep waters of your sorrow and find solace in the deepest streams of your love.

By its very nature, loss is love. If I did not love I would not find such devastation in loss. But love is not gone; never is love gone. In great loss, great hurt, great sorrow, life and love can appear to go missing. Our pathways in the Afterloss are here to find those missing pieces of life and resurface in this world with its greatest treasure – love.

Living in loss is also about putting the missing pieces back together, not like it was, but like it is – in a new mosaic. It is a different world that rose from the ashes of my Afterloss and I am not the same.

It is my deepest desire that you have found something here that has given you direction and depth in your travels in your Afterloss. We will meet again because we have met here. We will share our stories and find the story behind the story, the meaning within the lives that have touched us so deeply and will forever touch us. We will cry ancient tears freshly falling down our warm cheeks. And we will embrace in our pain, our joy, our sorrow, our solace, and most importantly, our love. For it is here we find the missing pieces of us are not missing in all. We will find in the expanse of life, in the midst of loss, the love that awaits us on every pathway.

A friend once told me, "If you are open to life, it will come to you." I truly believe that with all my being. I also truly believe if you are open to love, it will come to you. It is here we find the ones we will always love, still in love… and still loving. For in our openness to lean into wherever loss takes us, we will find our ultimate destination is the path itself – the pathway of love to love.

And on this pathway of love I have found that their lives here were not in vain. And my life here is not in vain. What they meant to me then still means the world to me now. The meaning of life truly is life itself.

Blessing upon you. Blessings upon us all.

Benjamin

About the Author

Several years ago Benjamin Allen appeared extensively in the media beginning with the *New York Times, Dateline, The Today Show, Good Morning America, 20/20* and various local newspapers, especially *The Dallas Morning News*. His story also featured on *The Oprah Winfrey Show*. The subject matter focused on the tragic circumstances his family endured.

Lydia, his wife, received a blood transfusion with HIV during the birth of their first child, Matt. He and Lydia had another child, Bryan, before they were informed of her infection. Consequently, his wife and their two children died, the first being in 1985 and the last death was in 1995.

In the midst of all this, one TV producer approached him to secure the rights to make a film about his life. He declined. Many people asked him to write his story, knowing how much it could potentially help others. He was not ready.

Finally, after many years of emotional and spiritual exploration, he came to a place of peace. His book, *Out of The Ashes: Healing in the Afterloss*, details that journey. Portraying normal people in abnormal circumstances, the book shows how he, and those he loved and lost, came to a deeper connection with life in the embrace of death.

It is an examination of what loss can take, but what it can also give. It is not a book about HIV/AIDS. It is a book that offers practical tips for dealing with any type of loss and moving into acceptance and healing.

Benjamin has worked with grieving individuals and groups for decades. He began his career as a Southern Baptist minister and was the pastor of Pacifica Baptist Church in California. He worked for the Christian Life Commission of the Baptist General Convention of Texas from 1985-1991. He was the founding Director of the Dallas AIDS Interfaith Network, and a member of the Texas Legislative Task Force on AIDS and the National AIDS Commission. From 1991-1995 he worked with the HIV Research Group at the University of Texas Southwestern Medical School in Dallas, Texas. Southwestern Medical School in Dallas, Texas.

His journey has brought him to a place of peace. As with everyone, Benjamin is still on the journey of healing. Once asked what he now believes, Benjamin responded, "I have no labels, no attachment to a particular belief. All I know is that I am a human, born of Spirit. And in Spirit, there is only love."

He now lives at Lake Tahoe, Nevada where he writes and delivers personal growth programs.

Please visit TheAfterLoss.com where Benjamin blogs regularly about the healing process. You can sign up there to receive more information and valuable resources. Join the active Facebook community at Facebook.com/theafterloss.

12959137R00085

Printed in Poland
by Amazon Fulfillment
Poland Sp. z o.o., Wrocław